THE JOURNAL OF BEATLES STUDIES

Autumn 2022

The Journal of Beatles Studies
Autumn 2022

Cover image: Detail taken from Shutterstock, stock
photo ID 667520851. Photo contributor: Lenscap Photography.

ISBN (Paperback) 9781802077667
Online ISSN 2754-7019

Publisher and Advertising
Liverpool University Press, 4 Cambridge Street,
Liverpool, L69 7ZU (telephone: +44 (0)151-794 2233;
email: lup@liverpool.ac.uk;
web: www.liverpooluniversitypress.co.uk).
Full details of advertisement rates can be obtained
from the publisher.

To advertise in *The Journal of Beatles Studies*, contact
Natasha Bikkul, Journals Marketing Executive,
at nbikkul@liverpool.ac.uk.

The Journal of Beatles Studies is hosted online at
https://www.liverpooluniversitypress.co.uk/r/beatles

Identification Statement
The Journal of Beatles Studies (online ISSN 2754-7019) is
published twice a year open access under a CC-BY licence
by Liverpool University Press, 4 Cambridge Street,
Liverpool, L69 7ZU.

Typeset by Carnegie Book Production, Lancaster.
Printed and bound by CPI Group (UK) Ltd, Croydon, CR0 4YY.

Contents

Reviews

Contributors

Christine Feldman-Barrett is Reviews Co-Editor of the *Journal of Beatles Studies*. She is Senior Lecturer in Sociology at Griffith University in Queensland, Australia. Her research focuses on youth culture history and she is the author of *A Women's History of the Beatles*, which was published by Bloomsbury Academic in 2021.

Dori Howard is a Kentucky-born, U.K.-based popular music studies researcher and writer. She holds a degree in the Beatles, Popular Music and Society and a PhD in Popular Music from Liverpool Hope University. She works at the Liverpool Institute for Performing Arts as a Teaching Fellow in Popular Music.

Steve Jones is UIC Distinguished Professor of Communication and Adjunct Professor of Computer Science at the University of Illinois Chicago, U.S.A. His research interests encompass popular music studies, music technology, sound studies, internet studies, virtual reality and human augmentics.

Clare Kinsella is Senior Lecturer in Criminology at Edge Hill University, Ormskirk, Lancashire, U.K. She has bachelor's and master's degrees from Lancaster University in Criminology and has a PhD from the University of Liverpool. She has published in a range of areas, including policing, homelessness and the concept of home, particularly in relation to Liverpool. Her most recent publication is a monograph, *Urban Regeneration and Neoliberalism: The New Liverpool Home*, published by Routledge in 2021.

Paul Long is Professor of Creative and Cultural Industries in the School of Media, Film and Journalism at Monash University in Victoria, Australia. He is Director of the Monash Migration and Inclusion Centre where he researches the role of migrants in the creative industries. He has published widely on music and media history, heritage and creativity, as well as on issues in cultural engagement and participation.

Richard Mills is Reviews Co-Editor of the *Journal of Beatles Studies*. He is Senior Lecturer in English, Creative Writing and Film & Screen Media at St Mary's University, London, U.K. Richard is the author

The Journal of Beatles Studies Autumn (2022)　　ISSN 2754-7019 (online)
https://doi.org/10.3828/jbs.2022.1

of *The Beatles and Fandom: Sex, Death and Progressive Nostalgia*, published by Bloomsbury in 2019.

Eleanor Peters is Senior Lecturer in Criminology at Edge Hill University. She has a PhD from the University of Bristol. Her main research interests are in the areas of youth and family justice and the relationship between music and crime. She has published in a number of journals including the *British Journal of Criminology*, the *International Journal of Social Research Methodology* and the *Journal of Social Welfare and Family Law*. Her most recent book is *The Use and Abuse of Music: Criminal Records*, published by Emerald in 2019.

Walter Podrazik is an Adjunct Lecturer at the University of Illinois Chicago, U.S.A. His research interests encompass television history, the intersection of politics and media, and narratives in popular music. He is co-author of three books on the Beatles.

Cass R. Sunstein is currently the Robert Walmsley University Professor at Harvard. He is the founder and director of the Program on Behavioral Economics and Public Policy at Harvard Law School. In 2018, he received the Holberg Prize from the government of Norway, sometimes described as the equivalent of the Nobel Prize for law and the humanities. In 2020, the World Health Organization appointed him as Chair of its technical advisory group on Behavioural Insights and Sciences for Health. From 2009 to 2012, he was Administrator of the White House Office of Information and Regulatory Affairs, and after that, he served on the President's Review Board on Intelligence and Communications Technologies and on the Pentagon's Defense Innovation Board. He has testified before congressional committees on many subjects, and he has advised officials at the United Nations, the European Commission, the World Bank and many nations on issues of law and public policy. He serves as an adviser to the Behavioural Insights Team in the United Kingdom.

Holly Tessler is Co-Editor of the *Journal of Beatles Studies*. She is Senior Lecturer in Music Industries and Programme Leader for the MA in Beatles, Music Industry and Heritage at the Institute of Popular Music, Department of Music, University of Liverpool. She created the University of Liverpool's first student-run record label, Merciful Sound. She is also a member of the Liverpool City Region's Beatles Legacy Group.

Introduction

In September of 2021, the *Journal of Beatles Studies* published a call for contributions to what you are presently reading: our inaugural issue. At the time, the world was eagerly anticipating the release of *The Beatles: Get Back*, Peter Jackson's eight-hour documentary series which undertook to recast the long-held dour narrative of the Beatles' final months together as presented in Michael Lindsay-Hogg's 1970 film, *Let It Be*. Following its release in November 2021, *Get Back* more than fulfilled its promise. Thanks to the technological wizardry of Jackson and his team, the grainy audio and video from the original footage, when restored, looked and sounded as if it could have been recorded last week, not more than half a century ago. The vitality of the visuals, the clarity of the audio and the palpable charisma of the Fab Four that was captured on film created a popular culture sensation last autumn, making social media stars of not only the Beatles themselves, but of people long relegated to the footnotes of Fab Four history: Glyn Johns and his flamboyant fashions; Mal Evans and his everyman affability; and Kevin Harrington's ineffable Jeeves-like presence. More substantially, *Get Back* deliberately sought to tell a more inclusive story than its predecessor. Here, we see the Beatles not in an isolated bubble but working amidst a constant stream of visitors. We see that they are friends, partners, collaborators, husbands, brothers and fathers: their creative exceptionalism proven not despite these external relationships but rather *because* of them. Scenes of the Beatles creating new music interspersed with quotidian vignettes of them drinking tea, eating jam butties and playing with their children foster in viewers a more human and down-to-earth conception of John, Paul, George and Ringo not as 'The Beatles' — larger-than-life characters in some fanciful fairy-tale myth — but as four young men whose sensibilities, beliefs and attitudes are remarkably like our own.

The Journal of Beatles Studies Autumn (2022)   ISSN 2754-7019 (online)
https://doi.org/10.3828/jbs.2022.2

In June 2022, as we finalize copy for this inaugural issue, Paul McCartney has just performed a two-and-a-half-hour headline set at England's Glastonbury Festival. Performing exactly one week after his eightieth birthday, much was made in media stories about McCartney being the oldest-ever solo headliner at Glastonbury, this year sharing the bill with 20-year-old Billie Eilish and 35-year-old Kendrick Lamar. McCartney's 38-song set included music that spanned almost the entirety of his career: from 'In Spite of All the Danger', a song he wrote in 1958, to tracks including 'Come on to Me' and 'Fuh You' from his second-most recent album, *Egypt Station*, released in 2018. The audience of around 100,000 seemed to grasp the significance of the moment, not only singing along to every song, but serenading McCartney with an impromptu version of 'Happy Birthday to You', which Macca seemed genuinely stunned to hear. Even special guests Dave Grohl and Bruce Springsteen appeared slightly in awe of the occasion, as both usually ebullient performers were instead content to be (comparatively) modest sidemen. In what might otherwise have been the most moving moment of the show, McCartney finished his set with 'Hey Jude', with the adoring crowd continuing the singalong even after Paul and the band had walked offstage. However, the real showstopper moment came in the encore, when McCartney performed a virtual duet of 'I've Got a Feeling' with John, via film footage of Lennon taken from Jackson's *Get Back* documentary. The performance created a palpably emotional experience, with both audience and performer overwhelmed by the magnitude of what they were witnessing: the now-octo-genarian Paul playing alongside the 28-year-old John, a Beatles reunion across space and time, in what was likely to be the last Glastonbury performance of McCartney's career.

What both *Get Back* and McCartney's headlining gig evidence is that even more than fifty years after their break-up, the Beatles remain a musical and cultural phenomenon. Perhaps somewhat counterintuitively, cultural and scholarly fascination with the Beatles has not diminished but flourished over time. More than a simple exercise in nostalgia, the Beatles, their music and particularly their story resonates just as much with today's Beatle 'twts' and 'stans' as with the original Beatlemania generation. How and why this is the case is a core concern of this journal. Scholarship about the Beatles is dizzyingly complex and diverse. There is, for instance, research on the Beatles and mathematics (Brown 2014) and the Beatles and electrical engineering (Zhou et al. 2018). In 2012, Z.V. Maizlin and Patrick Vos asked, 'Do we really need to thank the Beatles for the financing of the development of the computed tomography scanner?' (Spoiler alert: No, we don't.) The point being that, since the 1960s, there have been thousands of scholars, researchers and writers producing millions of words about myriad facets of the Beatles' lives and music. And each of these writers brings to their work expertise from a given field or discipline. Yet to date, beyond conferences, edited collections and fixed-term research projects, Beatles scholars have been working in comparative isolation, compelled to publish their findings for non-Beatles specialists and audiences. It is a situation that raises the question, why isn't there a field of Beatles Studies? Furthermore, what would it look like, who would define its agendas, methods, quality and potential, and to whom would it speak? This is a scholarly gap that the *Journal of Beatles Studies* seeks to redress. At its most elemental, the *Journal of Beatles Studies* will be a place, *the* place, for critical study, debate and discourse about the Beatles. It is not our intention to be prescriptive in our editorial approach as to what issues might shape and inform Beatles Studies. Instead, we endeavour to be the vehicle that allows scholars and writers to ask new questions about the Beatles, to help us understand why they have remained omnipresent in the popular and academic consciousnesses of the twentieth and twenty-first centuries.

Accordingly, the theme of this first issue is 'Navigating and narrating the Beatles: establishing a research agenda for the twenty-first century'. Through this idea we have sought contributions that explore how, why and through what means the Beatles are both subject and object of critical study. Our aim in doing so is to set in motion a forward-facing and dynamic framework not for *what* about the Beatles is being studied, but rather for *how* research might be undertaken, by whom and through what media and which channels. Thus, the first section of the journal features articles that seek to understand Beatles scholarship not as a celebratory and uncritical exercise in fact-finding or 'trainspotting', but as a means through which we can begin to answer the question of why the Beatles have remained a cultural constant, the focus of continuous evaluation and re-evaluation for more than half a century.

In the first article, Dori Howard takes an autoethnographic approach to both studying and teaching the Beatles within the U.K. Higher Education sector. Through her experiences of the first Beatles-focused postgraduate programme, Liverpool Hope University's MA The Beatles, Popular Music and Society, which ran from 2009 to 2019, Howard discusses how programme staff navigated the often-cynical popular perceptions of offering what was at the time seen as a 'Mickey Mouse' degree. Through detailed analysis of module content and the pedagogical approaches employed in the MA, she articulates how the MA established a Liverpool-centred community of scholarly practice where not only students and staff of the MA, but also visiting academics and researchers, as well as those people employed within Beatles tourism, have the means to interact, manage and reconceptualize the complex issues surrounding the group's Liverpool heritage and legacy. These enduring structural changes can be evidenced through the establishment of Beatles-focused enterprises including the Liverpool City Region's Beatles Legacy Group, the University of Liverpool's MA The Beatles, Music Industry and Heritage, as well as its Yoko Ono Lennon Centre and the *Journal of Beatles Studies* published by Liverpool University Press.

The complex and often contested issue of the Beatles' place in wider strategies of Liverpool heritage and cultural regeneration is discussed by Clare Kinsella and Eleanor Peters. Unpacking the connections between music, memory and place, the authors interrogate whether the economic and cultural benefit of being the only city in the world to be able to proclaim itself the Beatles' hometown has overshadowed the efforts of other Liverpool voices and other communities to tell their stories. Particularly in the period since the city's designation as 2008 European Capital of Culture, Kinsella and Peters question whether Liverpool has regularized and perhaps even sanitized the history of the Beatles' time in the city to fit a more convenient and marketable tourism and heritage narrative. Like Howard, Kinsella and Peters conclude that moving forward, a more discursive view is essential for keeping the Beatles' and Liverpool's heritage relevant to contemporary and diverse communities.

Steve Jones and Walter Podrazik take an approach to questions of Beatles history, legacy and narrative that is broadly akin to that of Kinsella and Peters, but which reaches a substantially different conclusion. In the context of their research Jones and Podrazik also view the story of the Beatles as something that is 'culturally, generationally, industrially and dynamically constructed' (p. 68). They argue that the ubiquity of new technologies and media has made it easier for the Beatles and their stakeholders to craft, fix and reinforce key moments of their history whilst downplaying others. This interaction between art and authenticity, fandom and commerce affords people with no personal lived history of the Beatles access to the group's story from multiple points of time, allowing them to pick and choose which aspects of the band's music, fashions, eras and beliefs are most compatible with their own interests and preferences. In this way, the real-life Beatles transform into 'The Beatles', musical, cultural and especially narrative icons whose value and meaning are adapted, reinterpreted and re-presented across time and generations.

Looking at the Beatles not as a musical group but as an enduring cultural phenomenon is an idea Jones and Podrazik share with our final contributor, Cass Sunstein. In his work, Sunstein asks the biggest Beatles question of all: why did the Beatles become a worldwide sensation? The simplest and perhaps most romantic answer is, he suggests, that the Beatles succeeded because of the self-evident quality of their music. But if considered from a more clinical point of view, Sunstein argues that the Beatles enjoyed the benefit of 'informational cascades'. Much like social media influencers, he writes that, 'People learn from others, and if some people seem to like something or to want to do something, others might like or do the same' (p. 104). Indeed, informational cascades seem a convenient means of describing how and why Beatlemania took hold of the world's youth in the 1960s. But are they alone a sufficient explanation for the Beatles' success? Via the concept of 'Lost Einsteins', Sunstein queries whether, if a different set of cultural, temporal and economic circumstances had prevailed, the world would have experienced a 'Kinksmania' or a 'Holliesmania' instead. Or were the Beatles truly one of a kind, emerging from the confluence of ability, fortuity and influence?

To produce a journal on the Beatles that only publishes scholarly research would be to exclude much of the important discourse and debate that is happening outside the academy. Thus, in the middle section of each issue of the *Journal of Beatles Studies* is a feature called 'Across the Universe', a place where Beatles-related news, performances, exhibitions, innovations and releases can be discussed. In this issue we feature two contributions. The first, from journal co-editor Paul Long, is a commemoration of Lizzie Bravo, the famed Apple Scruff who died on 4 October 2021. Through conversations with Lizzie's daughter Marya, Long shares anecdotes drawn from the detailed journals Lizzie kept throughout the three years she spent in London, hanging around outside Apple's Savile Row offices, culminating in John Lennon's invitation to Lizzie and another Scruff, Gayleen Pease, to come into the studio and sing backing vocals on the Beatles' recording of 'Across the Universe'. A central issue for this piece concerns the future of Bravo's memoir of her encounter with the Beatles and her life as a fan. Our second Across the Universe feature offers reflections on the music of Paul McCartney on the occasion of his eightieth birthday, 18 June 2022. A collective labour of love shared between the four journal editors, we have put together '80 at 80', a cooperative piece where each of us select twenty of our favourite McCartney songs and recordings. The different approaches we all took in completing the exercise is reflective not only of the depth and breadth of McCartney's catalogue but also of the varied and complex ways listeners engage, identify and connect with his music.

The final section of the journal features reviews of recently released Beatles media. In keeping with the remit of the journal, the materials selected for review are deliberately diverse. Allison Bumsted reviews Sibbie O'Sullivan's autoethnographic fandom account, *My Private Lennon* (Ohio State University Press, 2020); Luis Díaz-Santana Garza evaluates *Leadership Lessons with The Beatles: Actionable Tips and Tools for Becoming Better at Leading* by Shantha Mohan (Routledge, 2022); Taran Harris reviews the 2020 limited edition release of *John & Yoko/Plastic Ono Band*, edited by Simon Hilton (Thames and Hudson, 2020); and Michael R. Fisher reviews Paul McCartney's *The Lyrics: 1956 to the Present* (Liveright Publishing Corporation, 2021).

It is our intention for the journal to highlight new thinking and scholarship about the Beatles, particularly from writers with original perspectives and diverse views. Although limitations of space restrict how much we can publish in any issue, our aim is to reflect — and reflect upon — the ever-expanding field of activity which encompasses Beatles Studies. We are privileged to present to you our first issue of the journal.

Holly Tessler
University of Liverpool, U.K.
Holly.Tessler@liverpool.ac.uk

Paul Long
Monash University, Australia
paul.long@monash.edu

Co-Editors, the *Journal of Beatles Studies*

Bibliography

Brown, Jason I. (2004) 'Mathematics, physics and *A Hard Day's Night*', *CMS Notes* 36(6): 4—8.

Maizlin, Z.V. and P.M. Vos (2012) 'Do we really need to thank the Beatles for the financing of the development of the computed tomography scanner?', *Journal of Computer Assisted Tomography* 36(2): 161—164.

Zhou, Y., W. Chu, S. Young and X. Chen (2018) 'BandNet: a neural network-based, multi-instrument Beatles-style MIDI music composition machine', *arXiv preprint* arXiv:1812.07126.

Learning and teaching the Beatles

Experiences with Liverpool Hope's MA The Beatles, Popular Music and Society

Dori Howard
Liverpool Institute for Performing Arts, 49–51 Fleet Street,
The Jam Works, Apartment 15, Liverpool, L1 4AR
Dori.howard1@gmail.com

Abstract: This article considers Liverpool Hope University's Master of Arts degree in The Beatles, Popular Music and Society — which was the world's first academic degree specifically related to the study of the Beatles — through reflective investigation into its structure, pedagogy and foundation in popular music studies. Using the writer's own experiences as a both a graduate of and lecturer for the programme, the article considers the validity of academic study of the Beatles, the appropriateness of the MA's approaches to this study and the usefulness of these for current and future Beatles scholarship.

Keywords: Beatles, popular music studies, popular culture, popular music research, popular music education

The Beatles have been used within teaching and learning frameworks through many approaches, in many educational institutions, at many levels, for many types of students. In England specifically, the music of the Beatles is part of the national curriculum for primary students. Studying the life of John Lennon, as an example of a significant individual who has contributed to national and international achievements, is recommended as part of the history curriculum for age seven- to eleven-year-olds. At a further level, in 2015 the Assessments and Qualifications Alliance (AQA) added

The Journal of Beatles Studies Autumn (2022) ISSN 2754-7019 (online)
https://doi.org/10.3828/jbs.2022.3

Sgt. Pepper's Lonely Hearts Club Band as a recommended resource for the general certificate of secondary education (GCSE) in music (see AQA.org.uk 2022). Further, Paul O. Jenkins and Hugh Jenkins (2018: i) point to the many ways in which the Beatles have been used in higher education, including:

> treating the Beatles lyrics as poetry; their influence on the world of art, film, fashion and spirituality; the group's impact on post-war Britain; political aspects of the Fab Four; Lennon and McCartney's songwriting and musical innovations; the band's use of recording technology; [and] business aspects of the Beatles career[.]

This article focuses on what can be considered a crucial moment for the legitimization of the academic study of the Beatles in its formalization as the world's first academic degree specifically related to the study of the Beatles, the city of Liverpool and the Beatles tourism industry. Inaugurated in 2009 at Liverpool Hope University, the programme — a Masters of Arts entitled The Beatles, Popular Music and Society — was offered at the university for ten academic years and ended in 2019 following the departure of course director Dr Mike Brocken.[1] This article draws upon my own experiences — first as a student and then as a lecturer and module leader on the MA — to explore how the Beatles, the city they left behind and the music business they entered, together with the later Beatles-related tourist initiatives, were understood on the MA in terms of the academic study of popular music. The article also considers the precedent the course set for subsequent Beatles scholarship and pedagogy.

It must be stated that there are, of course, many valid approaches to the study of the Beatles. Similarly, there may be other graduates of the Beatles MA who would highlight different strands of their learning experience as equally important as the ones to which I draw attention in this autoethnographic article. After all, as George Lipsitz suggests, 'popular music is the "product

---

1. The Beatles, Popular Music and Society was offered at Liverpool Hope University from 2009–2019. It has no connection or affiliation to the MA The Beatles, Music Industry and Heritage currently offered at the University of Liverpool.

of an ongoing historical conversation in which no one has the first or last word"' (quoted in Negus 1996: 138). With that in mind, although my personal experiences with the Beatles MA have shaped and informed my own pedagogy, research and teaching, this article also incorporates reflections and work from graduates and instructors from different years of the programme's duration, presented with consent from those involved. Using these viewpoints, this article asserts that the study of the Beatles framed within the discipline of popular music studies taught on the MA provides useful consider-ations and methods for continued Beatles scholarship within higher education.

As someone whose professional life has mostly centred around the academic study of the Beatles, I often recall Paul McCartney's comments of 2014 about studying popular music with a focus on the Beatles. An American student in Liverpool for the MA programme had won tickets to a Q&A with McCartney in London and used the opportunity to ask for his opinion about the course. McCartney's response that it was 'ridiculous, and yet very flattering' made headlines, but he went on to suggest that using these courses to 'teach other people about [...] history', could be valuable (paul mccartney.com 2014). Indeed, approaches to teaching the Beatles within higher education have often stressed the value of using the group to provide a gateway for understanding various aspects of history in just this way. For example, Thompson (2018: 25) suggests that 'looking through the Beatles, we can see the roots of our current conversations about feminism, sexuality, drugs, war, class, privilege, and other aspects of our world shaped indelibly by events in the sixties'. Although the links to which Thompson points are useful in many ways depending on the course of study, it can be argued that such approaches to the band would benefit from a wider cast. Focusing solely on what the Beatles as a historical source can demonstrate about the past is indicative of a tendency within scholarship to view the Beatles as static historical figures representing a monolithic '1960s': as roots rather than as continually growing and changing. What about the teenager hearing her first Beatles song as a fifteen-second snippet on TikTok? What of the thousands of people employed in Beatles heritage tourism in Liverpool, London, or Hamburg whose working lives are affected by the modern-day implications of the past? What of the continuous recontextualizations of the Beatles' music taking place through covers, remixes and interpolation?

At the time of McCartney's comments about the MA, I received several emails from friends and family asking if I had been discouraged in my studies by his opinions. The answer lies in John Fiske's (1989: 104) suggestion that a popular music text can be understood as anything that can be imbued with meaning: music, images, and — I would argue — particularly performers that have reached the cultural status of the Beatles. He writes that popular music 'has loose ends that escape its control, its meanings exceed its power to discipline them, its gaps are wide enough for whole new texts to be produced in them — it is, in a very real sense, beyond its own control'. So, although the past is worthy of consideration and the Beatles a useful blueprint for investigating it, it is important to recognize that the Beatles are also very much a dynamic part of the present, and the value in studying this is one of the many significations of the Beatles that has perhaps escaped even McCartney's control.

However, for some in the U.K. in particular, the programme fell under the category of what has become known as a 'Mickey Mouse' degree, a term coined by U.K. Minister of State for Universities Margaret Hodge in 2003 and which was picked up and used by British media. Such courses, according to Hodge, involved 'content [that is] not perhaps as rigorous as one would expect and the degree may not have huge relevance to the labour market' (Woodward 2003). When the Beatles MA was announced in 2009, the press treated it as such a degree. An article in *The Guardian* described the MA as 'a course scrutinizing songs such as Octopus's Garden, While My Guitar Gently Weeps and I Want to Hold Your Hand', while also questioning what types of jobs the degree 'might yield in the current economic climate' (Jones 2009). Another headline — from the *New York Times* — quipped that it was a 'Masters in Paul-Is-Definitely-not-Dead' (Kozinn 2009).

However, as this article explores, Beatles scholarship is important in a variety of contexts for a variety of reasons, and the programme's foundation in popular music studies lies at the heart of its effectiveness, relevance and academic rigour. The methodologies associated with popular music studies manifest this in many ways: historical investigation uncovering 'hidden histories' outside of the traditional Beatles narrative to bring them into contemporary discourses; ethnographic research focusing on present-day Beatles audiences, businesses and tourism; semiotic analysis and communication studies taking account of pluralistic interpretations and meanings of the music of the Beatles; and so on. This article will explore these ideas in more depth, but it must first be established what is meant by popular music studies, an academic pursuit which itself has often been treated with suspicion.

Popular music studies

The growth and evolution of popular music studies as an academic discipline has been well documented (and debated) since its emergence from a dialogue between a multitude of disciplines. According to Bennett, Shank and Toynbee (2006: 5):

> Popular music studies has now emerged as a globally established and multi-disciplinary field. The international community of popular music scholars continues to grow, as does the range of specialisms that they bring to their work [...] the academic backgrounds of popular music researchers span a variety of disciplines, including musicology and ethnomusicology, anthropology, sociology, media and culture studies, politics, linguistics, history and English.

The research involved in popular music studies is mediated through several academic journals such as *Popular Music, Popular Music and Society*, and *The Journal of Popular Music Studies* (Bates 2013), and is supported by organizational research bodies such as the International Association for Popular Music (IASPM), which has branches in many parts of the world.

Focusing on undergraduate degrees, a 2012 report for the U.K.'s Higher Education Academy evidences the growing popularity of popular music studies within British higher education at the time, reporting that popular music degrees were offered at 47 institutions (Cloonan and Hulstedt 2012: 4). Of these 47 institutions, 27 were 'new Universities and 13 a mixture of University Colleges and Colleges, often post-dating 1992' (ibid.). Similarly, the majority of the programmes had been introduced after 2002, leading Cloonan and Hulstedt to suggest that popular music studies was a '"new" subject largely taught within "new" universities' (ibid.). It is important to point out that in the U.K., this sector, sometimes referred to as 'post-1992 universities' is distinct from traditional Russell Group universities which are often viewed as having a more rigorous focus on research and academic achievement. Previously polytechnics and colleges, post-1992 universities 'have had to typically carve out their own niche within the HE framework in the UK' (Chung 2018: 46) and have been associated with experiments in many new subjects such as media or popular music studies. These types of academic subjects have often drawn disdain from media commentators and politicians, as evidenced by the previous discussion of 'Mickey Mouse' degrees. Journalist Emma Brockes argued in 2003 that 'perfectly credible "new" degrees are undermined by their over-reliance on the word "studies" [...] anything with the word studies at the end of it is regarded by traditionalists as highly suspicious, in the same way that the word "flavour" in strawberry flavour drink, is used by the food industry to indicate something that's not quite the real deal' (Brockes 2003).

With these perceptions in mind, it is interesting to situate Liverpool Hope University and its Beatles MA within these findings. The smallest of the three major universities in Liverpool, Liverpool Hope is an amalgamation of three separate teacher training colleges. It was awarded 'new' university status in 2005, at which time Professor Gerald Pillay was appointed as Vice Chancellor (Hodges 2007). Pillay stated in 2007 that '[Liverpool Hope is] developing an international scholarly community, all research leaders in their own right' (Hodges 2007). That same year Brocken started as a full-time faculty member at the university. Brocken recalls how he was 'constructively thinking about starting an MA at the time', although the subject of the Beatles was not something he had initially envisioned:

I wouldn't have done a Beatles MA, to be perfectly honest [...] because I would have thought it was too narrowly focused. So, I wanted to start an MA rather similar to the one I'd studied, which was at the Institute of Popular Music at University of Liverpool. (Brocken 2022)

Brocken's idea was to structure the study of the Beatles as 'essentially a popular music studies MA in disguise' (Brocken 2022).

Pedagogy of the Beatles MA

Brocken's impulse and the pedagogy of the MA were framed by the discipline of popular music studies, which was set out clearly by him in the programme's handbook from the 2010/2011 academic year. He placed the MA in the context of an exponential growth in 'post WWII era popular music activity' which has been met with the emergences of a body of academic study concerned with key concepts regarding 'how popular success is determined, how popular music affects the lives and thoughts of people who create and hear it, and how popular music is historicized' (Brocken 2010: 7). He distinguished the MA from 'Several generic undergraduate taught courses on popular music', affirming the distinctiveness of this offer, suggesting that 'until now there has not existed a specific post graduate academic teaching and research-led programme co-ordinated by a university that considers the historical, contextual and musicological issues relating directly to the Beatles and their influence on popular culture and society up to the present' (ibid.).

Brocken goes on to suggest that the MA's focus on 'the music of the Beatles in the construction of identities, audiences, ethnicities and industries, and localities' will help students to 'understand popular music as a social practice, focusing attention on issues such as the role of music in the construction of regional identities, concepts of authenticity, aesthetics, meaning, value, performance, and the use of popular music as a discursive evocation of place' (ibid.).

The MA's four taught modules incorporated a variety of pedagogical strategies including lectures, seminars, presentations, independent reading and individual tutorials. They also included lectures by, and informal question and answer sessions with, local musicians, writers, entrepreneurs, tour guides and historians. Assessment methods included essays, presentations and, significantly, a small-scale ethnographic research project.

I move now into a discussion of the structure of the programme and individual modules on the Beatles MA. Whether studying full- or part-time, students experienced the modules in a particular order: 'Texts and Contexts: Understanding Popular Music', 'Topics in History: Representations of Liverpool', 'Cultural Musicology and the Beatles: The Sounds of Success', and 'Historical and Critical Approaches: Histories, Ethnographies and Tourism'. After completing these four modules, the final aspect of the programme was a dissertation of 12,000 to 15,000 words about an area of popular music related to the Beatles or wider subjects within popular music, which would be negotiated between Brocken and the student.

The following four sections discuss each module individually, drawing on information directly from the programme handbook. Although it is important to note that the handbook was continually updated throughout the duration of the programme, this article relies on the 2010/2011 handbook from the year I undertook the course. After exploring the handbook's information about coursework and learning outcomes, each section will provide critical reflections upon the approaches employed within the programme by detailing my own experiences with the modules, considering reflections from graduates of the MA, and discussing the links between the MA and current and future Beatles scholarship.

Each section begins with a summary of the module based on the information in the handbook along with its learning outcomes. Joanna Allan (1996: 93) suggests that learning outcomes in higher education 'represent what is formally assessed and accredited to the student', offering a 'viable model for the design of curricula in higher education which shifts the emphasis from input and process to the celebration of student learning'. The learning outcomes outlined in the Beatles MA handbook are interesting to consider and have been included in this article to further demonstrate the

MA's pedagogical approach, which views Beatles scholarship as involving qualitative considerations of consumption, social practice and signification rather than facts and figures to be memorized.

Texts and contexts: understanding popular music

According to the 2010/2011 handbook (Brocken 2010: 13), the 'Texts and Contexts' module introduced students to 'various theoretical standpoints and research techniques', and developed an understanding of 'key vocabulary and concepts' used within popular music studies. The foundations presented in this module provided 'an important opportunity for students to engage with concepts concerning the global and local importance of popular music production, reception and consumption' (Brocken 2010: 13). Specific case studies were incorporated into the module to highlight such issues in relationship to the Beatles.

The learning outcomes in the handbook suggest that students who had completed this module would be able to 'articulate a rigorous personal response to the interdisciplinary theoretical underpinning of Popular Music Studies' (Brocken 2010: 13). Second, they would be able to 'respond critically to a specific key concept and to apply this concept to a piece of designated written work concerning the Beatles', and lastly students could 'compare and connect social issues and historical debates in the study of the Beatles, popular music, and society' (ibid.).

As the entry module to the MA programme, content focused on key theoretical concepts often used within popular music studies including genre, authenticity, the music industry, gender and sexuality, music production and consumption, mediation, subcultures and scenes. According the handbook, 'the latter stages of the module will focus more closely on these popular music issues and how they directly involve the Beatles (such as influences, covering, authenticity, performance, locality, etc.)' (Brocken 2010: 14).

As a Beatles and music enthusiast who grew up in Kentucky, my undergraduate degree was in English and professional writing, and the existence of an entire academic discipline devoted to the study of popular music had never occurred to me. Even after moving thousands of miles to study the Beatles in Liverpool, on my first day of this module I was still unsure what this actually entailed even after close inspection of the handbook. Brocken would often tell students during this first module that we were not accepted on to the MA to 'sit around the campfire singing Beatles songs talking about how great they are'. This always painted an amusing image in my mind (and one which I suspect is not dissimilar to what my friends and family at home assumed was involved in my studies). Yet Brocken was not seeking to undermine absolutely the personal dedication to the band or our love for them that brought us together as students. In another study of such pedagogical practice, Punch Shaw (2021: 249) suggests that:

> one bit of baggage that a course based on the Beatles carries that should not be ignored is the fact that it is likely to be perceived as (gasp!) 'fun' [...] there should be nothing wrong with using pleasure as a teaching tool. But courses based on popular culture are often viewed by faculty and students as frivolous. For that reason, care must be taken in the design phase to build a certain amount of academic rigour in the course.

The 'Texts and Contexts' module set the academic standard for the rest of the MA. Like other more 'traditional' areas of academic study, the Beatles MA demanded student engagement with its own discipline-specific theories, terminology, methodologies and frameworks.

As an example of the academic rigour of the course, Melissa Davis, a lawyer from the US and a student from the first cohort in 2009/2010, recalls that 'once the lectures began, I found them to be not unlike those in law school with Mike's assignments [...] every bit as difficult as Secured Transaction Law. One of my classmates said at the end of one of his lectures [...]: "Now I'm going back to my room to lay down in the dark and cry"' (Davis 2022). My own experiences during the 'Texts and Contexts' module echo those of Davis: the terminology and concepts discussed were at times unfamiliar to me, requiring more reading and research outside of the classroom to fully grasp the content. However, tuition from Brocken — as well as the group discussions incorporated into the module — provided opportunities to unpack and consider some of the more challenging subjects. As Davis suggests, 'Mike made it all doable and always made himself available for a longer tutorial or an extra one, as needed. I came away feeling like it had been a worthwhile challenge that required a ton of work and was that once-in-a-lifetime experience I had hoped for all along' (Davis 2022).

Students were expected to read the work of important popular music studies writers and theorists such as Roy Shuker, Keith Negus, Sara Cohen, Tim Wall, Brian Longhurst, Philip Tagg, Marion Leonard and others. As a student on the MA, the readings helped me to recognize that popular music studies is a broad area of enquiry with scholars who move in and out of the field — providing interdisciplinary and multidisciplinary insights into different aspects of popular music. Later, as an educator on the MA, it was delightful to watch students new to the programme, and to popular music studies, discover new ways of looking at the world.

Neleigh Olson, a 2018/2019 student, likens the experience to being fitted with 'MA goggles' which helped her learn to 'see that so much of what we experience — history, the built environment, sound, art, music, genre, space and place, identity, authenticity, narratives — are [...] constantly shifting and informed by one another' (Olson 2022). She suggests that this realization helped to build upon her previous degree. Having completed an MFA in Creative Writing at the University of Kentucky prior to moving to Liverpool for the Beatles MA, Olson was interested in 'getting into nonfiction and researched-informed writing' and she credits the MA for developing her research skills. She says 'I left the program knowing how to be a theory-informed [...], nuanced and dogged Researcher with a capital "R." It's a skill that plays out across my academic, professional, and personal life like a switch I can't, and don't want to, turn off' (Olson 2022).

Equally, I found that students who did not fully engage with this module — the foundation of the entire MA — struggled with the subsequent modules, such as the 'Topics in History' module which followed. This again points to the academic standard expected of students. Far from being a 'Mickey Mouse' degree, the MA required research, reading, writing, engagement and understanding for successful completion of the programme.

Topics in history: representations of Liverpool

According to the MA's handbook, the 'Topics in History' module focused on the 'significance of British society and culture in the 20th century with specific concentration on the city of Liverpool and the role that such issues have played with regard to aspects of the Beatles careers' (Brocken 2010: 16). Using guest lectures, field trips and research, the module expected students to engage with ideas about 'musical production and consumption within the Liverpool of the post-WWII era and discuss the roles of locality, economics, race and identity, 'Americana' and space and place in the development of rock 'n' roll, jazz and skiffle specifically within the Merseyside region' (ibid.). The focus of the module on Liverpool and Merseyside in particular allowed opportunities for students to 'analyze various historical discourses surrounding the Beatles such as locality, cognition, power, regionality, and economics' (ibid.).

In terms of learning outcomes, after completing this module, the handbook suggests that a student should be able to 'integrate content, theory and methods for the interdisciplinary study of the Beatles' (ibid.). Secondly, students should be able to 'create hypotheses and problematise past and current debates in popular music histories, specifically those relating to locality and the Beatles'. Thirdly, students should be able to 'understand and demonstrate the relationship between research and the popular music past with specific regard to the career of the Beatles'. The final learning outcome suggested that students should be able to 'connect trends, social issues and texts and present, support and defend an informed position' (ibid.).

It has been suggested that much writing and study of the Beatles (whether academic, journalistic or fan-oriented) has been dominated by sets of culturally approved 'givens' that impact on their interpretation. Brocken (2016: 7) states that 'there has existed an entire body of constraints, a set of conventions, even within popular music fandom itself, that have "paraphrased" Beatles images and imaginings, authenticities and authorities into orthodoxies and traditionalisms of representation'. Brocken, writing with Melissa Davis (2012: 15), suggests that these types of 'given' understandings of the Beatles are 'historically questionable, for it leaves few spaces for arguments or interpretations, there is no room for polymorphic readings of contexts, there are in fact few joyfully erratic discoveries; we have, instead, the physical attestation of a victory for authorial space over thematic time'. It is apparent that Brocken and Davis are writing about what might be considered mythologies, mono-narratives or deterministic historical discourses surrounding the Beatles.

More recently, Christine Feldman-Barrett's book *A Women's History of the Beatles* (2021) identifies that, like much popular music historiography, the majority of recognized literature and discourse about the Beatles is limited by patriarchal constraints: a focus on male performers and male fans written by male writers. Outlining the work of writers such as Weber (2016) and Reddington (2012), Feldman-Barrett (2021: 2) suggests that 'the canon of Beatles literature – indeed the band's entire historiography – has been structured through male voices and sensibilities'. Additionally, Feldman-Barrett also asserts that Beatles fandom has been falsely cast 'as "White" and one situated with heteronormative rock culture' (2021: 44).

These types of historiography were explored in the 'Topics in History' module, which focused on written and visual representations of Liverpool over time to consider the Beatles, regionalism, space and locality. We read and considered non-scholarly Beatles texts from different eras, particularly biographies of the band and of individual members, and critically evaluated the story each one told of the band's relationship to Liverpool: how the narratives differed and how they stayed the same. It was fascinating to discover what Brocken and Davis (2012: 12) suggest is a 'litany of affirmation': the same pattern of events, the same emphasis on the same important figures and places, and the same meanings drawn from these that are repeated in many texts, many times, regardless of the veracity of some aspects of the narrative.

I found the MA's situation within Liverpool especially constructive for this module because it focused primarily on the mono-narratives, mythologies and historical discourses surrounding the Beatles and their relationship with the city. Melissa Davis has similar reflections:

> Living in Liverpool while going to school wasn't just fun or interesting or a culturally enriching experience; it enhanced the Beatles MA course of study. Walking in their city, going to church on Sunday at St. Peter's, concerts at the cathedral, everyday shopping, finding a dentist, walking through Sefton Park in all kinds of weather, Christmas shopping in the City Centre, even being hospitalized at the Royal (twice) all made me feel as though I knew them better (and the blood transfusions made me an honorary Scouser because it could truly be said I have Liverpool blood in me!). Would not trade the experience for anything and a remote [experience] — whether because of COVID or for convenience would not be the same. (Davis 2022)

I agree with Davis that undertaking this course anywhere other than Liverpool would not have delivered the same experience, education or understanding of the Beatles, and its location was one of the MA's greatest strengths. My own experience of living in the city during the MA helped me to question and deconstruct the patterns and mythologies embedded in the overarching historical narrative of 'the Beatles in Liverpool'. For example, many of the non-scholarly texts pointed to the working-class roots of the Beatles, particularly John Lennon. As a student from the U.S. with a different framework for understanding class-based connotations, I found the module's consideration of British society and culture useful for demarcating those differences and for understanding the significance of class both during the 1950s and 1960s and in present-day Britain. Although class is a complex concept to pin down, my MA cohort's scheduled visit to Mendips, John Lennon's large childhood home in the leafy Liverpool suburb of Woolton, gave me pause to consider the implications of blindly accepting John Lennon's label as a 'working-class hero' and the narratives that echo such claims.

Similarly, after an MA visit to the Casbah Coffee Club — a members-only club opened in 1959 in the cellar of Pete Best's family home in the West Derby area of Liverpool and where the Quarrymen often performed — one 2017/2018 student, Helen Maw, recognized that the historical discourses surrounding Merseybeat, in both contextual understandings and present-day tourist-based retellings, privileges the importance of the Cavern Club and Liverpool city centre as central to the development of Merseybeat and early Beatles fandom. Although this discourse holds value, she suggested in a work for the MA that leaving the Casbah (and its proprietor Mona Best) out of these early discourses related to the early Beatles is potentially problematic (Maw 2018). Brocken (2019) later built upon Maw's findings in an article for *Popular Music History* called 'Buildings matter', an example of the collaboration fostered by the MA's research community.

Recognizing and validating the existence of these overlooked or hidden histories is important within scholarship, not least because it adds to contemporary discourse surrounding the Beatles: it connects the past with the present day and raises questions about how the band can be understood — and by whom and for what purposes. Rodman (1999: 41) suggests that 'the beginnings of the stories we tell are actually the endpoints of *multiple* other stories that we don't have time or space to tell in full'. Such investigations illustrate the crux of what Tim Wall identifies as the difference between fan knowledge and scholarly knowledge. He argues:

> the best scholars reveal facets of popular music we were previously unaware of, analyse popular music culture and develop theories we can apply to help us understand in greater depth... Our job as scholars of popular music, then, is to analyse the conditions and practices of the production, textual form and consumption of music to understand how it is institutionalized, what its hidden assumptions are, and how the practices produce its meanings. (2013: xi–xii)

The 'Topics in History' module on the MA taught a crucial skill that I believe to be necessary for meaningful scholarship: the ability to recognize the existence of 'given' narratives associated with the

Beatles, to consider how these have been constructed and why, and to deconstruct them to reveal new avenues of understanding or interpretation.

Cultural musicology and the Beatles: sounds of success

According to the programme handbook, 'Cultural Musicology and the Beatles' focused primarily on the music of the Beatles through popular music semiotics. Using the work of popular music semiotician Philip Tagg, students were introduced to semiotic analysis using 'case studies surrounding the Beatles on film, studio sound production, lyric analysis and contemporary discourse analysis' (Brocken 2010: 18).

The first learning outcome upon completion of this module was that students should be able to 'develop specialised vocabulary, theory and methods for the analysis of popular music, including popular music on film' (Brocken 2010: 18). Second, they should be able to 'apply and refine critical thinking in relation to the study of popular music, and to apply this to the work of the Beatles', developing an ability to 'critically interpret, assess, compare and connect historical trends in sound production' (ibid.). Lastly, after completing the module they should be able to 'present and produce a written text employing a suitable popular music studies musicological typology' (ibid.).

Through the popular music studies theories and concepts discussed in the 'Texts and Contexts' module, students were introduced to the idea that there are many ways to approach meaning and communication within popular music performance and recordings beyond musicological expertise. This module dealt more specifically with the musical output of the Beatles than the other modules, and although there are many valid approaches to the analysis of the music, I recognize that my own background partially influences my championing of semiotics as a useful tool for analysis. Prior to the MA, I avoided the idea of studying any type of music academically because I was not a musician; I have no musical training or background in music theory. My initial concern when applying for the MA was that I lacked the foundations for what I imagined the study of the Beatles to be: analysis of their music and songwriting, requiring music theory. However, I found that analysis using the methodological approaches of structuralism and semiotics developed in popular music studies in the work of scholars such as Middleton and Tagg helped me to engage with the music of the Beatles in meaningful ways I had previously assumed impossible without an understanding of formal music theory. For instance, discussing the importance of semiotics as an appropriate method for popular music analysis, Tagg affirms the democratic opportunities of his pedagogy in his text *Music's Meanings*:

> When I started teaching popular music analysis to students with no formal musical training, I've seen repeated proof of great musical competence among those who never set foot inside musical academe. It's a largely uncodified vernacular competence that has with few exceptions been at best underestimated, more often trivialised or ignored, not only in conventional music studies but also by those individuals themselves. (2012: 5)

Semiotics certainly provided a language through which I could discuss the music and text – not simply its context. It is an avenue which deviates from many traditional approaches to teaching and learning about the music of the Beatles: ones which arguably often privilege musicology and assume knowledge of songwriting and music-making as requirements for accessing an understanding and appreciation of the musical output of the Beatles. For example, a 1963 *Times* (London) article, in which William Mann used the term 'aeolian cadence' to describe the harmonic progression in the song 'Not a Second Time', is often considered to be one of the first times popular music was described through classical music terminology, but certainly not the last (Capitain 2018: 143).

Although these traditional approaches are not without merit, as a non-musician popular music practitioner, a semiotic approach to popular music is now invaluable to me. However, as critical as I recognize it now to be, at that time – as a postgraduate student sitting in the 'Cultural Musicology and the Beatles' module learning about semiotics — I began to suspect that in terms of academic rigour and endurance, it probably would have been easier just to learn music theory instead. Of course, formal musicology has its own share of complicated terminology and learning curves. It could in fact be argued that for a degree focused on the study of popular music such as that of the Beatles, the drawback of a formal musicological approach is that its use of value-laden terminology, focus on notation, and an ideology framed by standards set by nineteenth-century European classical music (Middleton 1990: 104–106) attempts to define the very meaning of music based on these conventions. As I learned from speaking to other members of the MA research community about our shared interests, the music of the Beatles meant something different to each of us in our own ways. Because semiology highlights the importance of affect and communication processes, it suggests that the meaning of music is ascribed by individual listeners — musicians and non-musicians both — in the moment of reception and is therefore open to plural interpretations. Therefore, semiotics has proven to be an important tool within Beatles scholarship because it allows for consideration of such meaning potential without privileging certain types of knowledge or audiences over others, and aids consideration of the present-day interpretations generated by the music for a diversity of listeners within a myriad of contexts.

The specific, nuanced and pluralistic meanings generated by listeners and audiences is an aspect that is arguably often overlooked within the study of popular music. As Sara Cohen points out, 'it is still the case that assumptions are made about popular music practices and processes supported by little empirical evidence' (1993: 27); and I argue that this is still true today. The MA's last module before the dissertation, 'Historical and Critical Approaches', addressed this using ethnography, oral history and considerations of tourism.

Historical and critical approaches: histories, ethnographies and tourism

The 'Historical and Critical Approaches' module, according to the 2010/2011 handbook, was divided into three related sections. First, students continued to consider 'Beatles-related historiographies, primary and secondary sources' (Brocken 2010: 21). The second part involved studying ethnography and the Beatles, and part three gave students an introduction to issues 'from the contemporary Beatles tourist industry in Liverpool' (ibid.). Through these three parts, ethnography and oral testimony were 'introduced in depth to the researcher' (ibid.). For this module, students were expected to 'negotiate a research-based ethnographic/oral history project with their tutor' (ibid.).

In terms of learning outcomes, the handbook suggested that upon completion of the module, students should be able to 'work independently on a project involving the analysis and presentation of materials and issues relating to ethnographic research concerning the Beatles and Merseybeat' (Brocken 2010: 21). They should also be able 'utilise key methods and approaches surrounding the social anthropology of popular music' and to 'investigate, analyse and present findings concerning an issue of practical or policy-related relevance concerning the marketing of the Beatles' (ibid.). Finally, students should be able to 'Produce a presentation and report demonstrating a knowledge and understanding of a wide range of methods and approaches into understanding the reception and use value of popular music with specific relation to the Beatles, Merseybeat and Liverpool' (ibid.).

Unlike assessments for the other modules, which involved essays and presentations using primarily desk-based research, the 'Critical and Historical Approaches' module required that students 'get to know and involve themselves in the local Beatles histories, businesses, and industries and analyse oral testimony and the mythologies of place surrounding the Beatles' (ibid.). Students were asked to undertake an ethnography or oral history project which built upon concepts from other modules.

Sara Cohen (1993: 127) suggests that 'an ethnographic approach to the study of popular music, used alongside other methods (textual decoding, statistical analysis etc.) would emphasise that popular music is something created, used and interpreted by different individuals and groups. It is human activity involving social relationships, identities and collective practices.' This assessment meant that students were required to engage with considerations of how the meanings and function of the Beatles are manifest in contemporary cultural, social and economic contexts.

As a student, I enjoyed ethnographic research in particular, and my own ethnographic project for the MA investigated fan culture and Beatles-themed tattoos. After having spent much time on the 'Texts and Contexts' module reading and learning about the 'positive, personal, relatively deep, emotional connection[s fans can establish] with a mediated element of popular culture' (Duffett 2013: 2), it was fascinating to learn how these connections were described, understood and constructed by the people making them, in their own words. As in the 'Topics in History' module, I was often confronted with findings contrary to my initial expectations or personal interpretation. For example, a central assumption of my project was that tattoos are a permanent manifestation of fandom, yet one respondent challenged this by suggesting she planned to have her 'Let It Be' tattoo removed through laser surgery when she started a family. Additional findings in this ethnographic project revealed the nuanced and personal modes of consumption and identity construction that these tattoos represented: one participant's close relationship with his father who introduced him to the band, for example, or the desire of another participant to be seen as 'more invested' in the Beatles than other fans.

My involvement as an educator on the MA was predominantly on this module. I started by co-teaching one or two classes with Brocken, based on the tattoo ethnography project described. I eventually came to lead the 'Historical and Critical Approaches' module until the end of the degree programme in 2019. Throughout these years, Brocken often volunteered his own ongoing ethnographic research as teaching material (which investigated authoritative voices in Liverpool's Beatles tourism industry), and together we oversaw many interesting and innovative student projects. One example that stands out was a project through which a student initially intended to observe a café within a Liverpool Beatles tourist attraction to explore if it was patronized by locals in addition to tourists. What the student discovered through this process instead, however, raised questions about the lack of wheelchair access within Liverpool Beatles tourist attractions, leading her to question if the singular narrative of Beatles fans, in addition to being described as White and heteronormative, might also be described as excluding the disabled.

With each year, students interested in tourism-based ethnography projects became more and more predominant, and this, coupled with Brocken's own research at the time, led to a decision to transition the focus of the 'Historical and Critical Approaches' module to tourism and business. This anticipated more recent comments from Cohen (2020: 72) who has pointed to the need within Beatles scholarship for research relating to business and tourism, suggesting that 'for some time now The Beatles have been a focal point for debates concerning [Liverpool's] image and heritage and the development of its music and tourism industries, and although a vast amount of literature exists on The Beatles, little has been written on the ways in which they are used and discussed in contemporary Liverpool'. The MA's focus on both tourism and ethnography helped to recognize and address gaps in scholarship which require more in-depth consideration of the role and implications of the Beatles and their meanings and function in the present day.

The Beatles MA at Liverpool Hope integrated studies of contemporary practices and meaning into the programme through the partnership Brocken negotiated with The Beatles Story. The Beatles Story is a world-renowned tourist attraction at the Albert Dock in Liverpool, and employees were offered the opportunity of undertaking the MA programme. The first student to graduate with the master's degree as a result of the partnership with Liverpool Hope was Charlotte Martin in 2014. Martin had worked at The Beatles Story for close to two decades and was active in Liverpool as a green badge tour guide, accredited by the U.K. Institute of Tourist Guiding for her expertise about the city of Liverpool. Now running her own independent tour guiding service called LiverTours Liverpool, Martin (2022) remembers that 'the whole course, the whole environment I was in, it changed my life'. Martin had worked at The Beatles Story for nearly twenty years at the time she began the MA, and she suggests that the Beatles had become 'just a product to me'. However, she credits the MA for making the Beatles 'come alive again'. She says, 'Because I was learning different sides, different strands to how the boys [the Beatles] became who they were [...] I naturally fell back in love with them again', and she notes that she uses the insights gained from the MA in her tours (ibid.).

Inversely, it was interesting to witness how the presence of Martin and other students from The Beatles Story partnership provided students from non-tourism backgrounds with reminders that the Beatles were not only connected to historical considerations of the 1960s but also clearly connected to an economy and a pay packet for real, present-day people in their classes: a reminder of the Beatles' position within a profitable, present-day business model. These reflections are interesting when recalling Hodge's comments about 'Mickey Mouse' degrees and the need for 'relevance to the labour market' in higher education. Although formalized Beatles scholarship such as the MA can often be dismissed as frivolous, Martin's comments and experiences are linked to career progression, and the formation of her own tour guiding business after completing the MA is directly linked to the Liverpool tourism sector.

Dissertations, publications and career paths

The culmination of the MA was a 12,000–15,000-word dissertation written about an area of popular music, and many of the dissertations submitted throughout the programme are arguably emblematic of the effectiveness of the programme's pedagogical objectives and structure.

One such example by student Mary-Lu Zahalan from the 2009/2010 cohort uncovered a hidden history in examining the ways in which the Beatles 'broke' in Canada before they achieved success in the United States. This work was later expanded and published in 2011 as *Cultural Capital: The Beatles in Canada* by Beatleworks, a publisher set up by MA student Melissa Davis. Lindsey Eanet, a 2010/2011 student, investigated paradigms of authenticity familiar in popular music studies, in this case surrounding Danger Mouse's *The Grey Album* (2004), a 'mashup' or mix of Jay-Z's 2003 *The Black Album* and the Beatles' self-titled 1968 album (commonly referred to as the *White Album*). Eanet explored the implications of recontextualizations and rearticulations of the Beatles' music, as demonstrative of the varied, processual, contemporary meanings it can acquire in these instances of creative reuse and remaking (Eanet 2011). A merchandise manager for The Beatles Story, Hollie Durkin, who graduated from the course in 2018 supported by the MA partnership, investigated the early context and histories of Beatles tourism. Her work incorporated quantitative research to develop a projection for Beatles tourism in Liverpool based on her own experiences within the industry (Durkin 2017).

The MA also led directly to the publication of works initiated during the programme. Melissa Davis and Brocken collaborated on *The Beatles Bibliography* (2012), an annotated bibliography tool for researchers (with additional annotations contributed by MA student Angela Ballard). MA student Jeff Daniels and Brocken co-wrote *Gordon Stretton: Black British Transoceanic Jazz Pioneer* (2018) about the important musician from Liverpool. Numerous articles and book chapters have resulted from the research community cultivated by the programme, and several students, including myself, undertook doctoral study as a direct result of their experiences on the MA. One such student, Dr Esmee Hoek, now works as an international press contact for 70000 Tons of Metal, a heavy metal festival that takes place aboard a cruise ship; she says: 'I find in my current position, fans are highly active, and are part of a strong, international fan community [...] The course helped me gain an understanding of how people respond to popular music under different circumstances' (Hoek 2022). For other students, the MA has led to interesting (and sometimes unexpected) career trajectories that include heritage tourism, publishing, secondary and higher teaching, public speaking, podcasting and even the opening of a Beatles-themed creperie in France.

Conclusion

Returning to McCartney's 2014 comments about studying the Beatles, he said that '[The Beatles] never studied anything, we just loved our popular music [...] And it wasn't a case of studying it. I think for us, we'd have felt it would have ruined it to study it' (paulmccartney.com 2014). I can recall a student from my cohort echoing similar sentiments, as he questioned why the MA 'was trying to extract the magic from the unexplainable', and at the time I agreed with him at least to a certain extent. But the longer I have studied popular music, particularly the Beatles, the more I recognize that questioning and demystifying my own beliefs as a fan through scholarship creates a magic of its own through the creation of alternate knowledge, uncovered narratives and opportunities for new ways of viewing the readily familiar.

In formalizing the academic study of the Beatles through the first degree in the world dedicated to the band, the MA The Beatles, Popular Music and Society at Liverpool Hope University set a unique and well-considered framework for the study of the Beatles. Through its foundation in popular music studies and research-based teaching and learning, its contribution to the continued study of the Beatles is immense. The structure of the course, its pedagogy and the methodologies employed throughout offer the Beatles scholar creative and academically rigorous approaches through which to consider the band and its legacy in terms of both the past and present day. This was nurtured in pedagogies of historical investigation, seeking to uncover 'hidden histories' outside of the traditional Beatles narrative; through ethnographic research focusing on present-day Beatles audiences, businesses and tourism; through semiotic and structural methods which, I argue, are in and of themselves inclusive; and above all, through critical approaches which challenge deeply embedded mythologies regarding the Beatles, whether personally or culturally located.

The MA ran for ten academic years, ending in 2019 following the departure of Brocken. Although the programme is no longer offered at Liverpool Hope, it developed and fostered a research community that is still active, with many of us in regular contact about projects and ideas. Moreover, a crucial importance of the MA is that it served as a contact point for Beatles scholars from around the world who wished to research in Liverpool, providing an institutional network to connect and support Beatles researchers and scholars. After the programme's end, the absence of an institutional framework for such research left many scholars and potential scholars without a formal point of contact until the 2021 launch of The Beatles: Music Industry and Heritage MA at the University of Liverpool, which — although different from The Beatles, Popular Music and Society MA offered at Liverpool Hope — draws upon similar ideas discussed in this article in its aim 'to reframe and extend contemporary discourse about the Beatles beyond the historical and musicological into a broader and more robust 21st-century context' (liverpool.ac.uk n.d.). The current responses to and success of the University of Liverpool's MA, the *Journal of Beatles Studies*, and the Beatles Legacy Group established by the city of Liverpool in 2016 all evidence the validity of and continued need for scholarly consideration of the Beatles. It also evidences the impact of Liverpool Hope's MA The Beatles, Popular Music and Society which can be seen as a catalyst for such activity.

Bibliography

Allan, Joanna (1996) 'Learning outcomes in higher education', *Studies in Higher Education* 21(1): 93—108.

Bates, Eliot (2013) 'Popular music studies and the problems of sound, society and method', *IASPM Journal* 3(2):15—32, doi:10.5429/2079-3871(2013)v3i2.2en.

Bennett, Andy, Barry Shank and Jason Toynbee (2006) *The Popular Music Studies Reader* (Abingdon: Routledge).

Brocken, Michael (2010) *MA: The Beatles, Popular Music and Society 2009/2010 Course Handbook*. Unpublished.

Brocken, Michael (2016) *The Twenty-First Century Legacy of the Beatles: Liverpool and Popular Music Heritage Tourism* (Abingdon: Routledge).

Brocken, Michael (2019) 'Buildings matter: the recycling of Liverpool's Whitechapel and the Casbah', *Popular Music History* 12(1): 75–93, https://doi.org/10.1558/pomh.39559.

Brocken, Michael (2022) interviewed by Dori Howard (transcribed from audio recording), 19 December 2021.

Brocken, Michael and Jeff Daniels (2018) *Gordon Stretton: Black British Transoceanic Jazz Pioneer* (London: Lexington).

Brocken, Michael and Melissa Davis (2012) *The Beatles Bibliography: A New Guide to the Literature* (Manitou Springs: Beatleworks).

Brockes, Emma (2003) 'Taking the mick', *The Guardian*, 15 January 2003, https://www.theguardian.com/politics/2003/jan/15/education.highereducation (accessed 18 June 2022).

Capitain, Wouter (2018) 'Not a second time? John Lennon's aeolian cadence reconsidered', *Rock Music Studies* 5(2): 142–160, doi:10.1080/19401159.2018.1484613.

Chung, Jennifer (2018) 'Cultural shock of an international academic: from a liberal arts education in the United States to a post-1992 university in the UK', in *Academics' International Teaching Journeys: Personal Narratives of Transitions in Higher Education*, ed. Anesa Hosein, Namrata Roa, Chloe Shu-Hua Yeh and Ian Kinchin (London: Bloomsbury), 45–60.

Cloonan, Martin and Lauren Hulstedt (2012) 'Taking notes: mapping and teaching popular music in higher education', technical report for the Higher Education Academy, York.

Cohen, Sara (1993) 'Ethnography and popular music studies', *Popular Music* 12(2): 123–138.

Cohen, Sara (2020) 'More than the Beatles: popular music, tourism and urban regeneration', in *Tourists and Tourism: Identifying with People and Places*, ed. Don Macleod, Jackie D. Waldron and Simone Abram (Abingdon: Routledge), 71–90.

Davis, Melissa (2022) personal email to Dori Howard, 21 February 2022.

Duffett, Mark (2013) *Understanding Fandom: An Introduction to the Study of Media Fan Culture* (London: Bloomsbury).

Durkin, Hollie (2017) A consideration of the Beatles pound: a history, context and a projection of the economics of Beatles tourism in Liverpool. MA diss., Liverpool Hope University.

Eanet, Lindsay (2011) Whiter shades of grey: continuum and context in the popular music canon, from the Beatles' *White Album* to Danger Mouse's *Grey Album*. MA diss., Liverpool Hope University.

Feldman-Barrett, Christine (2021) *A Women's History of the Beatles* (London: Bloomsbury).

Fiske, John (1989) *Understanding Popular Culture* (London: Routledge).

Hodges, Lucy (2007) 'Small college, big hopes; UNIVERSITIES ++ Liverpool Hope — Europe's only ecumenical university — is resisting the urge to expand', *The Independent*, 28 June 2007, https://www.proquest.com/newspapers/small-college-big-hopes-universities-liverpool/docview/311316337/se-2?accountid=12116 (accessed 27 June 2022).

Hoek, Esmee (2022) personal email to Dori Howard, 3 March 2022.

Jenkins, Paul O. and Hugh Jenkins (eds) (2018) *Teaching the Beatles* (Abingdon: Routledge).

Jones, Sam (2009) 'The long and winding road to an MA in the Beatles songs', *The Guardian*, 4 March 2009, https://www.theguardian.com/education/2009/mar/04/beatles-higher-education-liverpool-university (accessed 4 February 2022).

Kozinn, Allan (2009) 'A master's in Paul-is-definitely-not-dead', *The New York Times*, 7 March 2009, https://www.nytimes.com/2009/03/08/weekinreview/08kozinn.html (accessed 1 February 2022).

Martin, Charlotte (2022) interviewed by Dori Howard (transcribed from audio recording), 17 February 2022.

Maw, Helen (2018) The Casbah and Mona Best: searching for the 'other'. MA diss., Liverpool Hope University.

Middleton, Richard (1990) *Studying Popular Music* (Milton Keynes: Open University Press).

Negus, Keith (1996) *Popular Music in Theory* (Cambridge: Polity).

Olson, Neleigh (2022) personal email to Dori Howard, 27 February 2022.

Reddington, Helen (2012) *Lost Women of Rock Music: Female Musicians of the Punk Era* (Sheffield: Equinox).

Rodman, Gilbert (1999) 'Histories', in *Key Terms in Popular Music and Culture*, ed. Bruce Horner and Thomas Swiss (London: Blackwell), 35—45.

Shaw, Punch (2016) 'The Beatles in the classroom: John, Paul, George and Ringo go to college', in *New Critical Perspectives on the Beatles: Things We Said Today*, ed. Kenneth Womack and Katie Kapurch (Basingstoke: Palgrave Macmillan), 243—262.

Tagg, Philip (2012) *Music's Meanings: A Modern Musicology for Non-Musos* (Huddersfield: The Mass Media Scholars Press).

Thompson, Gordon R. (2018) 'I'm looking through you: experiments in learning and the Beatles', in *Teaching the Beatles*, ed. Paul O. Jenkins and Hugh Jenkins (Abingdon: Routledge), 15–26.

Wall, Tim (2013) *Studying Popular Music Culture* (London: Sage).

Weber, Erin Torkelson (2016) *The Beatles and the Historians: An Analysis of Writings about the Fab Four* (Jefferson, NC: McFarland).

Woodward, Will (2003) '"Mickey Mouse" courses jibe angers students', *The Guardian*, 14 January 2003, https://www.theguardian.com/uk/2003/jan/14/highereducation.accesstouniversity (accessed 18 June 2022).

Zahalan, Mary-Lu (2011) *Cultural Capital: The Beatles in Canada* (Manitou Springs: Beatleworks).

Internet sources

AQA.org.uk (2022) 'Resource list: study pieces and listening list', https://www.aqa.org.uk/resources/music/gcse/music/teach/resource-list-study-pieces-and-listening-list (accessed 4 May 2022).

Liverpool.ac.uk (n.d.) 'The Beatles: Music Industry and Heritage MA', https://www.liverpool.ac.uk/music/study/postgraduate-taught/the-beatles-ma/ (accessed 29 May 2022).

Paulmccartney.com (2014) 'Impossible fan Q&A – four extra questions', 29 December 2014, https://www.paulmccartney.com/news/impossible-fan-qanda-four-extra-questions (accessed 4 May 2022).

'There are places I remember'

(Re)constructions of the Beatles as a Liverpool heritage object

Clare Kinsella
Edge Hill University, United Kingdom
kinsellc@edgehill.ac.uk

Eleanor Peters
Edge Hill University, United Kingdom
peterse@edgehill.ac.uk

Abstract: This article explores the relationship between music, memory and place, with specific reference to the centrality of the music of the Beatles, collective and individual, to the heritage industry in their birthplace, Liverpool. Since its emergence during the early 1980s, the cultural heritage sector in Liverpool has arguably relied heavily on its claim as the cradle of the genius of the Beatles, and it is thought in some quarters that more could be done to exploit this lucrative link. However, it is suggested here that causal links between the city of Liverpool and the inception and development of the Beatles are limited and tenuous, and, therefore, the (over-)reliance on the band by cultural regeneration professionals is based on a false claim. Further, it is argued that the Beatles story, as told and retold in this urban regeneration context, is a partial one which prioritizes some elements over others, mirroring the broader story of Liverpool as a heritage site.

Keywords: popular music culture, music tourism, urban renewal, nostalgia, event-led regeneration, narrative

The Journal of Beatles Studies Autumn (2022) ISSN 2754-7019 (online)
https://doi.org/10.3828/jbs.2022.4

Introduction

Since the 2003 announcement that Liverpool had won, against stiff competition, the accolade of European Capital of Culture (ECOC) for 2008 (Boland 2010), the city has been firmly established as a tourist destination. The city's maritime history, waterfront, architecture and cultural and artistic heritage are the key ingredients for a contemporary tourism offer which has been harnessed by business and local government alike to drive urban renewal and regeneration in a city previously ravaged by industrial decline and economic deprivation (Furmedge 2008; Kinsella 2021). Unsurprisingly, the Beatles, arguably the most significant cultural phenomenon of the twentieth century (Du Noyer 2012; Collins 2020), are placed front and centre in these processes: the jewel in Liverpool's cultural crown (McColgan 2015).

The purpose of this article is to explore the use of culture and heritage as drivers for urban regeneration in Liverpool, and the role that the Beatles play in these processes. Specifically, we argue that employment of the Beatles as a heritage object in the Liverpool context is very much partial as, in keeping with what is known about memory and tourism (Bartoletti 2010), the relationship between the group and Liverpool is reduced to a *partial* story. Nora (1989: 15) argues that 'the passage from memory to history has required every social group to redefine its identity through the revitalization of its own history. The task of remembering makes everyone his [*sic*] own historian.' A regularly recurring Liverpool Beatles narrative has been circulating through the city's formal and informal tourism and heritage sites, which emphasizes and prioritizes some elements, and downplays or even excludes others (Polkinghorne 1995; Zeller 1995; Kruse 2005; Erll 2011). Crucially, this dominant narrative is one which best supports the neoliberal, capitalist, urban regeneration goals of the tourism and heritage sector as successively envisioned by the governments of Thatcher, Major and Blair, respectively (cf. Hesmondhalgh et al. 2015; Hewison 2014; Long and Morpeth 2016); versions of the story which emphasize other forms of value are sidelined or even ignored. We articulate this by first establishing the relationship between music, nostalgia and tourism, and then exploring heritage tourism in Liverpool and where the Beatles sit within it. We consider how the story of the Beatles is regularly constructed and reconstructed according to how it will best support the dominant Liverpool regeneration narrative in a given period, and then close by considering what is lost when sanitized, glossy versions of the past are prized over the challenges of authenticity. As Johnson and Dawson, writing as part of the Centre for Contemporary Cultural Studies (CCCS) Popular Memory Group, suggest, historical memory often conforms to 'flattened stereotypes of myth' (Johnson and Dawson 1982: 12).

Music tourism and musical nostalgia

Music and tourism have often been associated, whether through operas attended during the European grand tours of the eighteenth and nineteenth centuries, or the importance of music in the nineteenth-century spa towns, such as Bath in England and Baden-Baden in Germany, where music became an integral part of the experience of a spa therapy (Bradley 2011). In Britain the growth of the railways helped the working classes to travel, particularly to seaside resorts which were closely tied to experiencing musical entertainment (Brennan 2015; Hughes and Benn 1998). Bradshaws, the producer of guidebooks, noted a great deal of tourism in Liverpool and the nearby seaside resort of New Brighton from the 1860s onwards (Bradley 2011), until the mid-twentieth century and the decline of many seaside resorts that was brought about by cheap international flights (Farr 2017). The New Brighton Tower opened in 1897 and attracted millions of visitors each year, providing leisure activities including ballroom dancing, acrobatics and orchestral concerts (Watt 2009). The Beatles played at the Tower Ballroom on twenty-seven occasions between 1961 and 1963 (Murphy 2011). The decline of the seaside resort in Britain is well documented (Farr 2017; Beatty, Fothergill and Gore 2014), and New Brighton was no exception to this, exemplified by photographer Martin Parr's depictions of the resort in the 1980s, particularly in

The Last Resort (Parr 2009). Since the turn of the century, New Brighton has undergone extensive regeneration, often drawing on its Edwardian heritage as well as its Beatles links (Nyland 2019).

As Lashua, Spracklen and Long (2014: 3) contend, 'music provides an important and emotive narrative for tourists, as an expression of culture, a form of heritage, a signifier of place and a marker of moments'. Brandellero et al. (2014) highlight that for the post-Second World War generation popular music might be a potent symbol of national or local identity and heritage. Nostalgia plays a part in this roster, described by Bartoletti as a 'typical modern illness' which manifests itself almost as homesickness for a time rather than a place, which can never really be regained (2010: 24). The value of music nostalgia has taken on increasing prominence, particularly among the post-war generation, in many aspects of life, including music, and Dauncey and Tinker (2014: para. 8) identify how this 'contributes to the development and status of particular popular music forms and genres', for instance quoting DeNora (2000: 63) on how music can be used as a process for remembering (or constructing) a person's identity and as 'a technology for spinning the apparently continuous tale of who one is'.

In an analysis of the psychology of cultural consumption, Schindler and Holbrook (2003) suggest that people can create nostalgic bonding through an interaction with a product at a crucial age — when the person is around twenty years old — and this can then create a lifelong preference for that object. Bennett (2001) highlights how popular culture's focus on 'retro' enables post-war generations to relive their (nostalgically represented) youth. Resonant in thinking about national identity, Collins (2020) pinpoints a sentimental view of Englishness in the depictions of the music and cultural impact of the Beatles to an idealized image of the sixties. Whether this is a nostalgic trip for those who lived through this period or for those who have come to it later, this sentiment is apparent in a number of phenomena. These include the mod revival of the 1970s, which reflected very closely the fashions, sounds and ideals of the 1960s subculture (Dow 2021); the resurgent career and then murder of John Lennon in 1980; and the Oasis-led Britpop era in the 1990s, which again looked back to an ideal of

1960s England (Kallioniemi 2016). Integral to this perspective is the continued omnipotence of the Beatles worldwide. As Penman (2021) states, the group are 'as much a part of the public conversation as they ever were' and Liverpool is the place where fans come to experience *their* Beatles and nostalgia.

Liverpool's contemporary heritage industry

Many contemporary cultural events in Liverpool reflect on the city's history, whether they are derived from its maritime heritage, for example the International Mersey River Festival (McColgan 2015), celebrate its music heritage, for example '50 Summers of Love' (Culture Liverpool 2017), or commemorate a particular anniversary, for example the First World War centenary celebrations (McColgan 2015). The Warwick Commission appears to take issue with such an approach and the role and motives of some of those behind such events:

> The role of cultural organisations as strategic partners in the more fundamental place-shaping role, building and moulding local communities and identities, remains underdeveloped. As a result, whilst the accounts of place that civic leaders give are often redolent of local pride and distinctiveness, the economic, cultural and social strategies that are seen to comprise place shaping often lack such distinctiveness, are based on *superficial 'famous dates and people'* idea [*sic*] of place identity or even disregard local cultural expression entirely. (Warwick Commission 2015: 66, emphasis added)

Reliance on 'superficial "famous dates and people"' is very much redolent of the recent approach adopted by Liverpool City Council and its partners (Kinsella 2021); we argue here that Liverpool's cultural heritage offering would be significantly diminished without recourse to a famous period associated with the city — the 1960s — and to arguably the best-known people associated with that period, the Beatles.

Kinsella has argued elsewhere (2021) that regeneration processes in the Liverpool context can be understood as reflecting two distinct trajectories, characterized as 'forward-facing' and 'backward-facing'. The 'forward-facing' era ranges from the end of the Second World War to the early 1980s, with a focus on the future of Liverpool expressed via modernization and physical expansion. The 'backward-facing' era, roughly starting from the 1980s onwards, focuses on Liverpool's industrial, commercial and cultural past via commemoration, heritagization and prioritization of the city centre.

To expand: the first period, when regeneration focused on the future, was based on the belief that Liverpool would continue to develop and prosper and, consequently, needed to be 'modernized' to cope with the demands of an increasing population, a strong workforce and a buoyant, flourishing economy. The second, 'backward-facing' era emerged towards the end of the 1970s. A disastrous decade for the city, this era represents an about-face in terms of understandings of where prosperity lay for Liverpool, and a 180-degree change of direction from prosperity based on an insecure, uncertain future, to prosperity based on a celebration of the city's past — its history, heritage and status as maritime city of empire.

Developing Kinsella's ideas further, we now examine key urban regeneration pushes in Liverpool from the 1960s, which assume a future characterized by economic boom, and the *volte-face* of the early 1980s towards a future based on the past. Crucially, we map these forward-facing and backward-facing processes against the evolution of the Beatles as a musical and cultural phenomenon, and their role as a source of both pride and angst in connection with the city's image and reputation.

Locating the Beatles against Liverpool's changing fortunes

The Beatles' story is among the best-known of popular music tales and is emblematic of the optimism and hope of the 'forward-facing' era of Liverpool's historical story. John Lennon and Paul McCartney met in 1957 in the Liverpool suburb of Woolton and along with George Harrison and others began to perform as the Quarrymen.

By 1962 John, Paul, and George were called the Beatles and were managed by local businessman Brian Epstein. They gained a new drummer, Ringo Starr. They released their first single, 'Love Me Do', and in 1963, *Please Please Me* became their first number one record in the U.K. This success was replicated first in the United States and then around the world. Gilmore (1994) articulates that the Beatles were seen as a force of energetic optimism in the U.S.A., where they arrived shortly after the assassination of President John F. Kennedy to a grieving country. As Lemonnier (2016: 46) writes, 'it is impossible to write a cultural and social history of the 1960s without mentioning the Beatles and recalling in passing their worldwide success.' More than just a popular music group, the Beatles were also culturally significant, symbolizing post-war Britain's changes, whether that be the 'invention' of the teenager and their consumerist behaviours (Savage 2010) or the intensification of social mobility in British society (Lawrence 2019), particularly in the North of England.

The initial connection of the orbits of McCartney, Lennon and Harrison in the late 1950s/early 1960s coincided with the first real signs of post-war urban regeneration in Liverpool. Couch (2003) notes that it was around this time that urban planning, or town planning as it was more commonly known in the U.K., came to be seen as a profession and a craft in its own right, alongside the emerging conceptualization of the city as a dynamic living organism. Thus, the town planning of the day was emblematic of a new dawn for urban life – it was planning for a bright, clean future – and very much reflected the economic and social optimism of the 1960s (Balderstone, Milne and Mulhearn 2014). Perhaps the best physical legacy of this futuristic, modernist optimism is St John's Beacon, built in the city centre in 1969 in an innovative space-age style (Muchnick 1970). This 400-foot-high tower, built in conjunction with St John's Precinct (shopping centre), incorporates a panoramic observation area which was originally constructed as a revolving restaurant that closed after just eight years (Kefford 2022). Now home to a radio station, the tower continues to contribute to the distinctive skyline of the city, in sharp contrast to the surrounding 'dingy' Georgian and Victorian cityscape (Tulloch 2011).

The modernist tone of the Liverpool *Interim Planning Policy Statement* (1964) and the *City Centre Plan* (1965) harnessed this optimism and 'civic confidence' (Murden 2006: 402) to envision a new city centre which would acknowledge concerns of both practicality and physical beauty (Couch 2003) and reject inner city low-level living in favour of high-rise tower blocks (Aughton 2008; Rogers 2010; Tulloch 2011). The dominant theme of building skywards is, for Tulloch, symbolic of the city's confidence:

> In the 1960s, additions continued to be made to the skyline as the city seemed to build ever upwards in a symbolic demonstration of masculine vigour, proclaiming to the world that Liverpool still had a lot to offer and those who thought the city was dead were in for a shock. (Tulloch 2011: 131)

Thus the future and prosperity of the city seemed assured, with new homes in the sky or in the suburbs fit for a new generation of workers employed in manufacturing at, for example, the newly established Ford Motor Company branch plant in Halewood — allowing for positive comparisons to be drawn between Liverpool and the original 'motor city', Detroit (Murden 2006), another hub of innovation and verve in terms of post-war popular music and culture (Posner 2002). For the city to be able to compete as a major player in the modern era, 'the ambition was to reshape and redevelop what was perceived to be an obsolete and inefficient city centre' (Couch 2003: 51).

This period of positivity, prosperity and hope in Liverpool coincided with one of the city's best-known eras, encapsulated in the term 'Merseybeat' (Jones 2020). The early 1960s saw a series of pop groups from the Liverpool music scene evoke a new energy in popular culture in the U.K. and find international fame and achieve cultural influence (Millington and Nelson 1986; Aughton 2008), which had the effect of bolstering the confident mood of a 'new prosperous Liverpool' (Frost and North 2013: 8). The Beatles were an integral part of the perceived positivity associated with the 1960s, a period of new fashions, art and an increase in economic prosperity. Arguably the creative and commercial success of Liverpool during this time, coupled with the futuristic and optimistic building programme, against a backdrop of presumed human progress and success epitomized by the excitement of the 'space race' (White 2015: 47), makes this period the zenith of forward-facing Liverpool, with great hopes for the future and where uncertainty was viewed as opportunity.

However, the optimistic hope for a brighter Liverpool life that characterized the climate of the 1960s was ultimately short lived. The early 1970s, whilst proving to be a difficult period for many British communities because of economic recession (Dow 1998), were positively catastrophic for Liverpool (Hayes 1987; Belchem 2006; Roberts 2010; Tulloch 2011; Balderstone, Milne and Mulhearn 2013; Frost and North 2013). The global recession of 1973 coincided with several other phenomena which rained heavy blows on the city. Liverpool's geographical location on the Mersey, once so advantageous to the city's prosperity and growth, was now at the root of its downfall. The continuing decline of the British empire (Belchem 2006), together with the U.K.'s commitment to the European Common Market (Murden 2006; Tulloch 2011), significantly reduced the amount of traffic and commerce through docks on the west of the country and, subsequently, the requirement for bulk processing industry dockside (Taylor 2009). Developments in the handling and transport of cargo, specifically the use of transport containers, rendered the docks to the south of the city obsolete (Belchem 2006; Balderstone, Milne and Mulhearn 2013).

Manufacturing industries in Liverpool have traditionally been characterized by what Heseltine and Leahy (2011: 22) refer to as 'branch plant syndrome', whereby large corporations' commitment to the city tended to comprise a single plant rather than wholesale operations and headquarters, largely because of an accepted view that the Liverpool workforce is both unreliable and 'strike-happy' (Murden 2006: 431). Arguably these ideas about Liverpool and Liverpudlians meant that the city bore the brunt of the economic decline of the 1970s and its impact on business and industry in the U.K., as firm after firm withdrew from their weakest point by closing down branch plants (Grady 2014). Mass unemployment and mass depopulation of Liverpool were the result (Hayes 1987).

Thus, by the 1970s the city had a post-industrial landscape characterized by decay, dereliction and abandonment. A discourse of self-inflicted demise was attributed to the population of Liverpool by critics, deflecting attention away from the many and varied structural causes of decline over which the city's inhabitants had no control (Topping and Smith 1977; Belchem 2006). A significant proportion of young male inhabitants, in a bid to kill time created by unemployment, turned to drugs; cannabis at first, then through lack of availability, heroin (Pearson and Gilman 1994; Thornton 2003). These addictions were fed in many cases through crime (Fazey 1988; Pearson 1991). A further aspect of the multi-faceted 'unique' nature of 'problem Liverpool' arose as a result of Liverpool Football Club's success in European competition, which brought its supporters to continental destinations where they obtained, either by purchasing or through theft, designer sportswear not available in the U.K. (Thornton 2003). This led to a developing close association in the popular imagination between football, crime, violence, gang culture and Liverpool (Lawrence and Pipini 2016).

By the early 1980s the devastation started by the decline in industry dating back to the 1960s was virtually complete, and Liverpool's identity as a post-industrial city became firmly entrenched (Roberts 2010). The inner-city disturbances of the summer of 1981 compounded the near universal view that the city was beyond redemption. This is arguably best encapsulated in this oft-cited opinion piece published in the *Daily Mirror*: 'They should build a fence around [Liverpool] and charge admission. For sadly it has become a "show-case" for everything that has gone wrong in Britain's major cities' (quoted in Coleman 2004: 105). The 'fence' called for by this journalist was never built; however, their suggestion of making a spectacle of the city came to pass in a way, since largely as a result of the intervention of the unofficial 'Minister for Merseyside' Michael Heseltine, and in the aftermath of John Lennon's death, Liverpool's future was identified as its becoming a centre of culture, leisure and tourism (Crick 1997; Robson 1988; Lawless 1989; Couch 2003; Tulloch 2011; Feldman-Barrett 2021).

Early initiatives designed to spark regeneration through culture and heritage included the redevelopment of the central yet long defunct Albert Dock (a site listed by Historic England as having Grade I status, meaning that it is a structure of exceptional interest), the hosting of the 1984 Tall Ships Race, the opening of the International Garden Festival in 1984 and, crucially, the opening of the Beatle City exhibition in Seel Street in the same year (Couch 2003; Wiener 1986; Robson 1988; Lawless 1989; Tulloch 2011). In the early 1990s, the arrival and 'kicking in' period of Objective 1 funding[1] – awarded by the European Union to areas where gross domestic product per head is less than 75% of the European Union average (Jones and Skilton 2014) – coincided with several grassroots developments which had the impact of bringing revenue to, increasing the 'brand' of, and, crucially as it turned out, showcasing the *culture* of Liverpool. The first Mathew Street Festival, a loosely Beatles-themed free outdoor music event in the city's Cavern Quarter, was held during the August bank holiday weekend of 1993, and attracted 20,000 spectators (Wright 2015). Meanwhile, following nascent attempts at establishing music venues such as Quadrant Park and 051, James Barton opened Cream, a night club which sought to reject the seedy, dangerous image of the old 'clubland' and fill a void in Liverpool's music scene with a bespoke site dedicated to dance music. Cream would very quickly establish a reputation for a 'Scouse house' scene, which would attract coachloads of revellers from around the country (Du Noyer 2002: 221). Thus, the long-standing local recognition of Liverpool as a 'party town' (Murden 2006: 479) began to be disseminated further afield.

Heseltine and Leahy (2011) note that periods of regeneration tend to come in waves. Arguably, events such as the Mathew Street Festival and the birth of the Cream franchise, together with the push and support of European funding, marked the starting point of a wave of rebirth and redevelopment which paved the way for contemporary regenerative processes, cultural revival and event-driven regeneration (Couch 2003; Coleman 2004). 'Heritage tourism' (Timothy 2011), which acknowledges and celebrates buildings, artefacts, traditions and 'famous children' (Furmedge

---

1. Merseyside's initial Objective 1 funding period ran from 1993 to 1999. The area was granted a second period of funding from 2000 to 2006 (Gripaios and Bishop 2006).

2008: 89), was identified by local government as a central and vital feature of the 'mega regeneration' (Tallon 2013: 197) that Liverpool needed. The crucial element of heritage tourism in the Liverpool case, the driving force that would set the city apart from other places blighted by post-industrial decline, was identified as 'culture' (Coleman 2004; Aughton 2008; Tallon 2013). This was exemplified by the opening of the Museum of Liverpool Life in 1993 (Moore 1997) and also the Rope Walks project which saw the renovation and spotlighting of long, narrow streets in the Bold Street area that were initially constructed to facilitate the making of maritime rope (Bayley 2010). In retail, the development of the Queen Square complex (Boland 1996) was enabled; and in transport, the overhaul of the Gyratory and Paradise Street bus station. Public safety and surveillance were addressed through the wholesale installation of closed circuit television cameras (CCTV) across the city centre in the wake of the abduction and murder of James Bulger (Coleman 2004). What all of these disparate developments shared, though, was a focus on consumption and a commitment to private investment (Couch 2003; Coleman 2004; Tallon 2013).

Millennial Liverpool

The contemporary Liverpool characterized by its offer of heritage, culture and ostentatious consumption was fully consolidated in June 2003, when the ECOC accolade, by which the European Commission identified Liverpool as a centre of rich cultural heritage, was announced. The people of Liverpool were reported to be intensely proud of this achievement, which would act as a counterbalance to, and a rebuttal of, the persistent negative reputation that the city struggled to shake off, as well as being a useful source of revenue (Allt 2008; Furmedge 2008; Boland 2010; Cox and O'Brien 2012). Music tourism, related to the city's famous past, and in particular the Beatles, was offered as a fundamental cornerstone to this consolidation of cultural regeneration (Cohen 2007). Intrinsic to this is the acknowledgement that, without music, Liverpool would have little to offer as a cultural centre: Mike Wilkinson, when he was head of Liverpool's tourism, arts and heritage department, emphasized this strategy, stating 'when you ask foreign visitors what they knew about the city before they came here, it boils down to football teams and pop groups' (Wheeller 1996, quoted in Connell and Gibson 2002: 226–227).

Unsurprisingly, the Beatles have been front and centre among the football teams and pop groups (Cohen 2007; Lashua 2011). The first Beatles statue in the city, 'Four Lads Who Shook the World' by Arthur Dooley, was erected in Mathew Street in 1974. It features a Madonna-like figure with outstretched arms holding swaddled infants, representing Liverpool as the mother (city) of the Beatles. The original sculpture depicted John, George and Ringo as the babes-in-arms while Paul was represented as a baby with wings (this element was stolen and then returned years later). The sculpture was altered following John Lennon's death with the words 'Lennon Lives' added (*Liverpool Echo*, 2005).

From this inauspicious beginning there has been a growth in tourist-oriented uses of various Liverpool locations: souvenir shops, the Beatles Story Museum, hotels with Beatles themes and an 'authentic' replica Cavern Club (Connell and Gibson 2002). The Beatles' childhood homes have been protected (some might argue, exploited) via the National Trust, which is a heritage conservation organization. The reconstruction in 1984 of the '1960s Cavern' opposite the original site of the Cavern Club, which had opened in 1957 and closed in 1973 to accommodate a ventilation shaft (Leigh 2015), is also an exercise in heritage revision and protection.

Despite this contemporary focus on the Beatles as being integral to Liverpool's heritage narrative, it is important to remember that the band left the city for London in 1963, and it is arguable that much of their later development both as a musical group and as individuals owes a lot to the capital's 1960s scene rather than their hometown (MacDonald 2007). The group's association with various London locations has also been exploited for Beatles tourist heritage sites, most notably the famous Abbey Road zebra crossing depicted on the iconic 1969 album cover (Jones n.d.), which is now officially designated as a site of particular historic and/or architectural significance.

Returning to Merseyside music tourism, it is interesting to consider that there were originally tensions between those music fans who wanted to preserve the Liverpool legacy of the Beatles, and the city administrators who felt investment should be in the city's future, not its past (Brocken 2016). The influence of the public and public interest groups in establishing the memories and artefacts as part of heritage practices concerning the band was vital to this period of Beatles heritage in Liverpool (Leonard and Strachan 2010). The original drive for representations of the Beatles in Liverpool was predominantly fan-led, because plans for a statue were rejected by the city authorities as being unworthy of a place in the history of Liverpool. At some points in their career, the Beatles were seen to have brought discredit on the city. A *Daily Mail* article in October 1974 reported on a Liverpool City Council meeting where there was a discussion about whether a statue of the Beatles should be erected in the city. The article reads:

> The Beatles have been disinherited by heads of the city [...] Councillors in Liverpool branded John Lennon, Paul McCartney, George Harrison and Ringo Starr as a 'discredit' to their birthplace [...] Tory councillor, Tony McVeigh, added, 'The Beatles couldn't sing for toffee. Their behaviour brought tremendous discredit to the city. John Lennon returned his MBE medal to the Queen. It was an absolute insult.' (quoted in Badman 2009: 1977)

As this extract from the popular tabloid press illustrates, the meaning and importance of the Beatles was often in dispute throughout the 1960s and 1970s (MacDonald 2007). Collins (2020) identifies how the Beatles appeared unthreatening in the early 1960s; for example, they appeared before the Queen Mother at *The Royal Variety Show* in 1963 and received honours in the form of MBEs in 1965.[2] However, their association with the social and cultural changes of the era, for example experimentation with drugs and countercultural politics, led to indignation and outrage

---

2. The awarding of the Member of the Order of the British Empire was not without controversy at the time (Collins 2020). As a protest about the U.K.'s support for the Vietnam war, John Lennon returned his MBE in 1969 (Inglis 1996).

from politicians and parts of the media. Those once-provocative acts of the Beatles have, over time, somewhat lost their shock value in some quarters as opinions have changed through the years, with these transgressions encompassed by more partial and nostalgic memories of the 1960s. There is a cleaning up of the past in Liverpool's depiction of the Beatles. Post break-up, the group grew in prominence within the city's culture, and a Beatles music tourism industry has been constructed that offers new interpretations of the past and recreates the city of Liverpool as a symbolic place that claims to authentically represent the group. However, the marketing of places involves a manipulation of discourses, where some dominate and others are sidelined (Kruse 2005). Each member of the Beatles was a creative human being with complex personalities and complicated lives; arguably this nuance and intricacy is overlooked in this context.

We would argue that the resulting narrative focus on the Beatles' career in Merseyside is one in which they are carefully (and commercially) remythologized (Kruse 2005). It is largely nostalgic and romantic because the dominant discourse of the band used to represent places in Liverpool emphasizes youth and playfulness — that is, their early 1960s emergence in the city. This privileging of certain discourses is most notable in the reimagining of John Lennon, no doubt influenced by his murder in 1980 (Barnett 2020). Liverpool John Lennon Airport was the first airport in the United Kingdom to be named after an individual, a major acknowledgement of the importance of the tourist market to Liverpool. The iconography, and the tagline 'above us only sky' from the song 'Imagine', represents Lennon as a poet, privileging this particular discourse regarding his reputation while ignoring other, more controversial depictions, including radical politics, drug taking and domestic violence (Barnett 2020; Kruse 2005).

The avoidance or ignorance of particular aspects of the Beatles story raises valid questions about the authenticity of the version of the band presented in heritage discourse to galvanize tourism and the experience economy (Long, Cantillon and Baker 2022). As Kruse (2005: 89) identifies, the narratives that are promoted are 'highly selective, generally accessible and lacking in controversy'.

The commodification of experience and the presentation of artistic and literary places as tourist attractions are often disputed by those who experienced them first hand (Kinsella 2021) and by those who are represented (Badman 2009). As Brocken (2016: 209) argues, such commodifications and presentations are 'contingent on questions concerning fundamental civil, political, ethical and cultural roles in both popular music and cities in our time'.

Nostalgia, the Beatles and the notion of 'story'

As Radstone (2010: 188) notes, 'nostalgia has been associated both with a melancholy and conservative response to modernity's uncertainties' and this can be seen in the way the Beatles have been depicted by the tourist industries. Tourists visit Penny Lane simply to have their photograph taken alongside the street sign, as there is nothing else there of note. Strawberry Field, the site of a former children's home, only opened to the public for the first time in 2019 (Strawberry Field n.d.). Strachan (2010) argues that the Beatles' nostalgia is suburban, and they themselves are reminiscing about a previous, already diminishing Liverpool, that of the suburban 1950s.[3] As with all memories, the events might arguably never have actually happened and rather are reconstructed and reshaped, and represent an idyll and a desire to return home that can be seen particularly in Beatles songs such as 'Penny Lane' and the original lyrics to 'In My Life'.[4]

3. This is a recurring theme in Peter Jackson's 2021 documentary series *The Beatles: Get Back*, where the Beatles revisit songs from their early career and experiences in Liverpool.
4. John Lennon's original lyrics to 'In My Life' include mention of a number of Liverpool landmarks seen from the deck of the number 5 bus from his suburban house into the city, including a mention of Penny Lane. Lennon apparently changed the lyrics to be less Liverpool-specific as he said it sounded like a boring bus trip (Brewer 2021). McCartney's later song 'Penny Lane' delivers a suburban trip down memory lane, while 'Strawberry Fields Forever', despite being another suburban memory, named after a Liverpool orphanage, is a particularly otherworldly trip.

When Joe Anderson was Liverpool City Mayor between 2012 and 2021, he reportedly believed that Liverpool did not do enough to celebrate its status as the home city of the Beatles and saw this as a potential further historic area to exploit (McColgan 2015). This is, however, part of a wider trend of a 'memory industry' (Erll 2011: 3) and, more specifically, 'memory tourism' (Bartoletti 2010: 23). Drawing on Pierre Nora's conceptualization of *lieux de mémoire* as sites of collective memory, Erll recognizes that collective memory is a social construction, in that what we are encouraged to remember is delivered or revealed to us via 'specialised carriers of tradition' (Erll 2011: 29) who are authorized to establish 'official' memory as opposed to 'vernacular' memory. Thus, a process develops whereby what we remember and what we forget becomes politicized, in that what is deemed memory-worthy is dictated by the powerful. Drawing on Derrida's (1995) concept of 'archival fever', Erll identifies 'a contradictory drive, or desire, to collect and remember and at the same time to repress, destroy and forget' (2011: 51). It is possible to use Erll's analysis to explain event-led regeneration in Liverpool: Liverpool City Council and its partners act as 'specialised carriers of tradition' (ibid: 29), deciding what to remember and establishing the city's waterfront, or St George's Plateau, as the designated site for remembering.

Nostalgia — memories of, and affection for, previous times — is essentially selective and subjective. When something is perceived as deserving of heritage status it is afforded a certain gravitas; a level of dignity, respect and reverence that cannot be attributed in the same way to other phenomena. Because Liverpool as a city has an abundance of history and heritage, feelings of importance, significance and pride facilitate a deep and widely held love for those aspects of the city revered as valuable, distinctive and evidential of a glorious past. Nostalgia about the post-war period acted as a diversion from the social and economic deprivation in the city in the 1970s and 1980s and, from a regeneration perspective, as a way of glossing over it (Mayne 2017).

There is a recognition that narrative and life history are essentially social and cultural constructions (Polkinghorne 1995; Fielding

2006), not least because memory also shares these characteristics (Woodside 2010). Emihovich, for example, states that 'stories do not pretend to be objective because they deal with emotions, the irrational part of behaviour, they tap into qualities of imagination and fantasy' (1995: 39). Bowler (2019) argues that whenever a Beatles location in Liverpool is discussed, arguably other, potentially more important histories of the city are going to be overlooked, whether this be its mercantile and nautical heritage, or the legacy of the city's prosperity built upon the slave trade. The Beatles often cast a shadow over contemporary Liverpool musicians, with many Liverpool bands described as 'the next Beatles'. Thus, it could be argued that Liverpool's 'other' heritage(s) have been overshadowed by a nostalgic fondness for the group and the excitement and promise of Liverpool of the early 1960s.

Conclusion

Liverpool's past is now established, in a variety of ways, as central to both its present and projections of its future identity. Crucially though, only certain versions of, or elements within, the past are validated as 'culture' and 'heritage' worthy of commemoration and commercialization. The Beatles were a bigger mainstream act and commercial success than other Liverpool bands — either during their years of activity or compared to those who came after (Echo and the Bunnymen, for example) — thus they are worthy of commemoration. The Everyman Theatre was successful, but small and intimate — thus, rather than being conserved it had to be redeveloped for an audience of 400 and its old seats auctioned off as mementos (BBC News 2011). The Pier Head had a night-time 'scene' beloved of locals, but it was depriving business of making capital out of the views over the Mersey — thus it had to be remodelled with hotels and restaurants. The past is constructed as vital to Liverpool's future prosperity, but some elements of the past are deemed either not worthy or not profit making; therefore, they are airbrushed from the version of the past prioritized and co-opted by 'the regeneration professional' (Furmedge 2008:

82). The specific emphasis on the Beatles drowns out important alternative scenes in Merseyside, including black and minority ethnic communities (Bowler 2019). It also downplays other cities' significant influence on the development of the group, for example Hamburg. Fremaux and Fremaux (2013: 1) state that Hamburg's role has been overshadowed by 'cultural ownership of the band that was claimed by Liverpool's tourism industry in the 1980s and 1990s'.[5] In this sense, Liverpool's centring of the Beatles as the jewel in its cultural heritage crown is something of a false claim.

The way Beatles tourism manifests itself in Liverpool is simplified and one-dimensional; focus is placed on their early relationships with each other and their initial successes. Other than Lennon, whose murder in 1980 invoked homage to what might be called his 'Imagine' period, little attention is paid to the solo careers of the Beatles, meaning that the greater part of the 1970s is missing from the Liverpool account of Beatles-based nostalgia. This mirrors broader Beatles fandom which associates the 1970s with bad blood between the former group members and the increasingly diminishing likelihood of a reunion (Badman 2009). It also, however, mirrors broader cultural and tourism-driven regeneration narratives in Liverpool, which attempt to draw a veil over the 1970s as a most difficult era for the city, and a 'blip' in terms of culture and the arts, even though other, relatively less commercially successful, scenes flourished in Liverpool during this time. While the deaths of John Lennon and later George Harrison, coupled with much-publicized visits 'home' by Paul McCartney and Ringo Starr, have allowed for more consideration of them as individuals, it is the early 1960s Beatles that are most prevalent in how they are depicted in Liverpool tourism.

Both of the present article's authors re-engaged with the Beatles via various methods in preparation for writing this article. Peters, for example, in watching the eight hours of Peter Jackson's *The Beatles: Get Back*, observed frequent references to their Liverpool pasts scattered throughout. Kinsella, meanwhile,

5. This is true, although in 2009 the city of Hamburg opened the Beatlemania Museum in the Reeperbahn area of the St Pauli district.

gained first-hand experience of Beatles tourism in Liverpool by going on the *Magical Mystery Tour* excursion, which departs from the Albert Dock and ends with free entrance to the Cavern Club. Having been a regular at the club between approximately 1989 and 1993, when the venue had been split into two areas — one featuring music from the 1950s through the 1970s along with contemporary 'indie' hits, the other devoted to the emerging dance music scene — she was shocked to discover all evidence of this latter period in the venue's history obliterated, replaced with various Merseybeat memorabilia. This vignette captures the essence of our argument here. Cultural heritage, when packaged as a singular narrative to support regeneration drives, is essentially selective — plot points, instigating incidents and turns of events are chosen on the basis of *how well they support the chosen version of events,* as opposed to how reflective they are of a messy and contentious reality. Thus, use of the Beatles as a device to drive regeneration is partial — focused on four talented madcap moptops and a hint of colourful psychedelia, and ignoring, for example, sexual infidelity, drug use, imprisonment, accusations of blasphemy, Lennon's 'lost weekend', and various other controversies (Everett and Riley 2019). A gesture to a challenging authenticity is sacrificed in favour of saleability.

Acknowledgements

The authors would like to thank the anonymous referees and the editors for their helpful comments.

Bibliography

Allt, Nicky (2008) 'Sintroduction', in *The Culture of Capital,* ed. Nicky Allt (Liverpool: Liverpool University Press), 1—8.
Aughton, Peter (2008) *Liverpool: A People's History,* 3rd edn (Lancaster: Carnegie Publishing).
Badman, Keith (2009) *The Beatles: Off the Record,* ii: *The Dream is Over* [ebook] (London: Omnibus Press).

Balderstone, Laura, Graeme J. Milne and Rachel Mulhearn (2014) 'Memory and place on the Liverpool Waterfront in the mid-twentieth century', *Urban History* 41(3): 478–496, doi:10.1017/S0963926813000734.

Barnett, David (2020) 'How John Lennon was made into a myth', *BBC Culture*, 8 December 2020, https://www.bbc.com/culture/article/20201207-how-john-lennon-was-made-into-a-myth (accessed 22 February 2022).

Bartoletti, Roberta (2010) '"Memory tourism" and commodification of nostalgia', in *Tourism and Visual Culture*, i: *Theories and Concepts*, ed. Peter Burns, Cathy Palmer and Jo-Anne Lester (Wallingford: CABI Publishing), 23–42.

Bayley, Stephen (2010) *Liverpool: Shaping the City* (London: RIBA Press).

BBC News (2011) 'Liverpool's Everyman Theatre auctions seats', 28 July 2011, http://www.bbc.co.uk/news/uk-england-merseyside-14328526 (accessed 8 April 2017).

Beatty, Christina, Steve Fothergill and Tony Gore (2014) *Seaside Towns in the Age of Austerity* [report]. Centre for Regional Economic and Social Research, Sheffield Hallam University, Sheffield, U.K.

Belchem, John (2006) *Merseypride: Essays in Liverpool Exceptionalism* (Liverpool: Liverpool University Press).

Bennett, Andy (2001) *Cultures of Popular Music* (Milton Keynes: Open University Press).

Boland, Philip (1996) 'Institutional mechanisms and regional development in Merseyside: Objective 1 status', in *Regional Development Strategies: A European Perspective*, ed. Jeremy Alden and Philip Boland (Abingdon: Jessica Kingsley), 107–128.

Boland, Philip (2010) '"Capital of culture — you must be having a laugh!" Challenging the official rhetoric of Liverpool as the 2008 European cultural capital', *Social & Cultural Geography* 11(7): 627–645, doi:10.1080/14649365.2010.508562.

Bowler, Megan (2019) 'Liverpool: a city overshadowed by the Beatles?', *The Gale Review* [blog], 10 April 2019, https://review.gale.com/2019/04/10/liverpool-a-city-overshadowed-by-the-beatles/ (accessed 12 May 2022).

Bradley, Ian (2011) *Water Music: Making Music in the Spas of Europe and North America* (Oxford: Oxford University Press).

Brandellero, Amanda, Susanne Janssen, Sara Cohen and Les Roberts (2014) 'Popular music heritage, cultural memory and cultural identity', *International Journal of Heritage Studies* 20(3): 219–223, doi:10.1080/13527258.2013.821624.

Brennan, Matt (2015) 'The musical lives of British seaside piers', *The People's Pier* [blog], 26 October 2015, https://blogs.brighton.ac.uk/thepeoplespier/2015/10/26/the-musical-lives-of-british-seaside-piers (accessed 12 May 2022).

Brewer, Mark R. (2021) *Because: A Fan Picks His Top Forty Songs by the Fab Four* (Bloomington, IN: Xlibris Publishing).

Brocken, Mike (2016) *The Twenty-First Century Legacy of the Beatles: Liverpool and Popular Music Heritage Tourism* (Aldershot: Ashgate).

Cohen, Sara (2007) *Decline, Renewal in the City in Popular Music Culture: Beyond the Beatles* (Aldershot: Ashgate).

Coleman, Roy (2004) *Reclaiming the Streets: Surveillance, Social Control and the City* (Cullompton: Willan).

Collins, Marcus (2020) *The Beatles and Sixties Britain* (Cambridge: Cambridge University Press).

Connell, John and Chris Gibson (2002) *Sound Tracks: Popular Music Identity and Place* (London: Taylor & Francis Group).

Couch, Chris (2003) *City of Change and Challenge: Urban Planning and Regeneration in Liverpool* (Aldershot: Ashgate).

Cox, Tamsin and Dave O'Brien (2012) 'The "scouse wedding" and other myths: reflections on the evolution of a "Liverpool model" for urban regeneration', *Cultural Trends* 21(2): 93–101.

Crick, Michael (1997) *Michael Heseltine: A Biography* (London: Penguin).

Culture Liverpool (2017) '67–17: 50 Summers of Love', https://www.cultureliverpool.co.uk/summer-of-love/ (accessed 8 May 2017).

Dallen, Timothy J. (2011) *Cultural Heritage and Tourism: An Introduction* (Bristol: Channel View Publications).

Dauncey, Hugh and Chris Tinker (2014) 'Introduction: popular music nostalgia' [electronic version in English], *Volume! La revue des musiques populaires* 11(1), OpenEdition Journals, https://doi.org/10.4000/volume.4202.

DeNora, Tia (2000) *Music in Everyday Life* (Cambridge: Cambridge University Press).

Derrida, Jacques (1995) *Archive Fever: A Freudian Impression*, trans. Eric Prenowitz (Chicago: University of Chicago Press).

Dow, Christopher (1998) *Major Recessions: Britain and the World, 1925–1995* (Oxford: Oxford University Press).

Dow, Todd (2021) The migration of mod: analysing the mod subculture in the North of England. MA thesis, University of Huddersfield.

Du Noyer, Paul (2002) *Liverpool: Wondrous Place: Music from the Cavern to the Coral* (London: Virgin Books).

Emihovich, Catherine (1995) 'Distancing passion: narratives in social science', in *Life History and Narrative,* ed. Amos J. Hatch and Richard Wisniewski (Abingdon: Routledge Falmer), 37–48.

Erll, Astrid (2011) *Memory in Culture,* trans. Sarah B. Young (Basingstoke: Palgrave Macmillan).

Everett, Walter and Tim Riley (2019) *What Goes On: The Beatles, their Music and their Time* (New York: Oxford University Press).

Farr, Martin (2017) 'Decline beside the seaside: British seaside resorts and declinism', in *Mass Tourism in a Small World,* ed. David Harrison and Richard Sharpley (Wallingford: CABI), 105–117.

Fazey, Cindy (1988) *The evaluation of Liverpool drug dependency clinic: The first two years 1985–1987* [report to Mersey Regional Health Authority] (Liverpool: Research Evaluation and Data Analysis).

Feldman-Barrett, Christine (2021) *A Women's History of the Beatles* (New York: Bloomsbury).

Fielding, Nigel (2006) 'Life history', in *The Sage Dictionary of Social Research Methods,* ed. Victor Jupp (London: Sage), 159–161.

Fremaux, Stephanie and Mark Fremaux (2013) 'Remembering the Beatles' legacy in Hamburg's problematic tourism strategy', *Journal of Heritage Tourism* 8(4): 303–319.

Frost, Diane and Peter North (2013) *Militant Liverpool: A City on the Edge* (Liverpool: Liverpool University Press).

Furmedge, Peter (2008) 'The regeneration professionals', in *The Culture of Capital,* ed. Nicky Allt (Liverpool: Liverpool University Press), 82–92.

Gilmore, Mikal (1994) *Stories Done: Writings on the 1960s and its Discontents* (New York: Free Press).

Grady, Helen (2014) 'The English city that wanted to "break away" from the UK', BBC News Magazine, http://www.bbc.co.uk/news/magazine-29953611 (accessed 8 April 2016).

Gripaios, Peter and Paul Bishop (2006) 'Objective One funding in the UK, a critical assessment', *Regional Studies* 40: 937–952.

Hayes, Michael G. (1987) *Past Trends and Future Prospects: Urban Change in Liverpool 1961–2001* (Liverpool: Liverpool City Council).

Heseltine, Michael and Terry Leahy (2011) *Rebalancing Britain: Policy or Slogan? Liverpool City Region – Building on its Strengths: An Independent Report* (London: Department for Business, Innovation and Skills).

Hesmondhalgh, David, Melissa Nisbett, Kate Oakley and David Lee (2015) 'Were New Labour's cultural policies neo-liberal?', *International Journal of Cultural Policy* 21(1): 97–111.

Hewison, Robert (2014) *Cultural Capital: The Rise and Fall of Creative Britain* (London: Verso).

Hughes, Howard and Danielle Benn (1998) 'Holiday entertainment in a British seaside resort town', *The Journal of Arts Management, Law, and Society* 27(4): 295–307.

Inglis, Ian (1996) 'Ideology, trajectory & stardom: Elvis Presley & the Beatles', *International Review of the Aesthetics and Sociology of Music* 27(1): 53–78.

Johnson, Richard and Graham Dawson (1982) 'What do we mean by popular memory?' [discussion paper], Popular Memory Group, Centre for Contemporary Cultural Studies, University of Birmingham, http://epapers.bham.ac.uk/view/series/CCCS_Stencilled_Occasional_Papers=3A_History_Series.html.

Jones, Melanie and Louise Skilton (2014) 'An analysis of labour market outcomes in the European Union Objective One funding area in Great Britain', *Regional Studies* 48(7): 1194–1211.

Jones, Michael (2020) 'The place of the Beatles within Liverpool as a UNESCO City of Music', in *Music Cities*, ed. Christina Ballico and Allan Watson (London: Palgrave Macmillan), 81–101.

Jones, Richard (n.d.) 'The Beatles Abbey Road Crossing: Be a daytripper in north London', London Walking Tours [website], https://www.london-walking-tours.co.uk/secret-london/the-beatles-abbey-road-crossing.htm (accessed 8 February 2022).

Kallioniemi, Kari (2016) *Englishness, Pop, and Post-war Britain* (Bristol: Intellect Press).

Kefford, Alistair (2022) *The Life and Death of the Shopping City: Public Planning and Private Redevelopment in Britain Since 1945* (Cambridge: Cambridge University Press).

Kinsella, Clare (2021) *Urban Regeneration and Neo-liberalism: The New Liverpool Home* (Abingdon: Routledge).

Kruse, Robert J. (2005) 'The Beatles as place makers: narrated landscapes in Liverpool, England', *Journal of Cultural Geography* 22(2): 87–114, doi:10.1080/08873630509478240.

Lashua, Brett (2011) 'An atlas of musical memories: popular music, leisure and urban change', *Leisure* 35(2): 133–152.

Lashua, Brett, Karl Spracklen and Paul Long (2014) 'Introduction to the special issue: music and tourism', *Tourist Studies* 14(1): 3–9.

Lawless, Paul (1989) *Britain's Inner Cities*, 2nd edn (London: Paul Chapman Publishing).

Lawrence, Jon (2019) *Me, Me, Me: The Search for Community in Post-war England* (Oxford: Oxford University Press).

Lawrence, Stefan and Magdalin Pipini (2016) 'Violence', in *Studying Football*, ed. Ellis Cashmore and Kevin Dixon (Abingdon: Routledge), 11–29.

Leigh, Spencer (2015) *The Cavern Club: The Rise of The Beatles and Merseybeat* (Carmarthen: McNidder and Grace).

Lemonnier, Bertrand (2016) 'The Beatles, an "object of History"', *Volume!* 12(2): 45–53.

Leonard, Marion and Rob Strachan (eds) (2010) *The Beat Goes On: Liverpool, Popular Music and the Changing City* (Liverpool: Liverpool University Press).

Liverpool Echo (2005) 'Mud is all you need to repair Paul', 16 September 2005, https://www.liverpoolecho.co.uk/whats-on/music/mud-you-need-repair-paul-3527788 (accessed 19 June 2022).

Long, Paul, Zelmarie Cantillon and Sarah Baker (2022) 'Conceptualizing popular music's heritage as an object of policy: preservation, performance and promotion', in *Bloomsbury Handbook of Popular Music Policy*, ed. Shane Homan (New York: Bloomsbury), 73–90.

Long, Philip and Nigel Morpeth (eds) (2016) *Tourism and the Creative Industries: Theories, Policies and Practice* (Abingdon: Routledge).

MacDonald, Ian (2007) *Revolution in the Head: The Beatles' Records and the Sixties*, 3rd edn (Chicago: Chicago Review Press).

Mayne, Alan (2017) *Slums: The History of a Global Injustice* (London: Reaktion Books).

McColgan, Claire (2015) 'Place making on the waterfront', paper read at Liverpool International Waterfront Forum, Liverpool, 3–4 June.

Millington, Bob and Robin Nelson (1986) *'Boys from the Blackstuff': The Making of TV Drama* (London: Comedia).

Moore, Kevin (1997) *Museums and Popular Culture* (London: Cassel).

Muchnick, David (1970) *Urban Renewal in Liverpool* (Birkenhead: The Social Administration Research Trust).

Murden, Jon (2006) 'City of change and challenge: Liverpool since 1945', in *Liverpool 800: Culture, Character and History*, ed. John Belchem (Liverpool: Liverpool University Press), 393–485.

Murphy, Liam (2011) 'Plaque unveiled to mark the Beatles connection with historic New Brighton Tower Ballroom', *Liverpool Echo*, 21 November 2011, https://www.liverpoolecho.co.uk/news/liverpool-news/plaque-unveiled-mark-beatles-connection-3360719 (accessed 31 May 2022).

Nora, Pierre (1989) 'Between memory and history: *Les lieux de mémoire*', *Representations* 26: 7–25.

Nyland, Matthew (2019) 'More plans for New Brighton regeneration', JMU Journalism, 10 October 2019, http://jmu-journalism.org.uk/more-plans-for-new-brighton-regeneration (accessed 6 March 2022).

Parr, Martin (2009) *The Last Resort* (Stockport: Dewi Lewis Publishing).

Pearson, Geoff (1991) 'Drug-control policies in Britain', *Crime and Justice* 14: 167–227.

Pearson, Geoff and Mark Gillman (1994) 'Local and regional variations in drug misuse: The British heroin epidemic of the 1980s', in *Heroin Addiction and Drug Policy: The British System*, ed. John Strang and Michael Gossop (Oxford: Oxford University Press), 102–120.

Penman, Ian (2021) 'Four moptop yobbos', *London Review of Books* 43, 17 June 2021, https://www.lrb.co.uk/the-paper/v43/n12/ian-penman/four-moptop-yobbos (accessed 31 May 2022).

Polkinghorne, Donald E. (1995) 'Narrative configuration in qualitative analysis', in *Life History and Narrative*, ed. Amos J. Hatch and Richard Wisniewski (Abingdon: Routledge Falmer), 5–23.

Posner, Gerald (2002) *Motown: Music, Money, Sex and Power* (New York: Random House).

Radstone, Susannah (2010) 'Nostalgia: home-comings and departures', *Memory Studies* 3(3): 187–191.

Roberts, Les (2010) 'World in one city: surrealist geography and time-space compression in Alex Cox's Liverpool', *Tourism and Visual Culture* 1: 200–215.

Robson, Brian (1988) *Those Inner Cities: Reconciling the Social and Economic Aims of Urban Policy* (Oxford: Clarendon Press).

Rogers, Ken (2010) *The Lost Tribe of Everton and Scottie Road* (Liverpool: Trinity Mirror Media).

Savage, Jon (2010) *Teenage: The Creation of Youth* (London: Pimlico Press).

Schindler, Robert M. and Morris B. Holbrook (2003) 'Nostalgia for early experience as a determinant of consumer preferences', *Psychology and Marketing* 20(4): 275–302, doi:10.1002/mar.10074.

Strachan, Rob (2010) 'From sea shanties to cosmic scousers. The city, memory and representation in Liverpool popular culture', in *The Beat Goes On: Liverpool, Popular Music and the Changing City*, ed. Marion Leonard and Rob Strachan (Liverpool: Liverpool University Press), 43–64.

Strawberry Field (n.d.) 'Visit', https://strawberryfieldliverpool.com/visit (accessed 16 June 2022).

Tallon, Andrew (2013) *Urban Regeneration in the UK*, 2nd edn (Abingdon: Routledge).

Taylor, David (2009) *Liverpool: Regeneration of a City Centre* (Manchester: BDP).

Thornton, Phil (2003) *Casuals: Football, Fighting and Fashion: The Story of a Terrace Cult* (Preston: Milo Books).

Topping, Phil and George Smith (1977) *Government against Poverty? Liverpool Community Development Project 1970–75* (Oxford: University of Oxford Social Evaluation Unit).

Tulloch, Alex (2011) *The Story of Liverpool* (Stroud: The History Press).

The Warwick Commission (2015) *Enriching Britain: Culture, Creativity and Growth* [report] (Coventry: University of Warwick).

Watt, Paul (2009) 'A "gigantic and popular place of entertainment": Granville Bantock and music-making at the New Brighton Tower in the late 1890s', *Royal Musical Association Research Chronicle* 42: 109–164.

Wheeller, B. (1996) 'No particular place to go: travel, tourism and popular music, a mid-life crisis perspective', in *Tourism and Culture: Towards the 21st Century: Conference Proceedings*, ed. Mike Robinson, Nigel Evans and Paul Callaghan (Sunderland: Centre for Travel and Tourism and Business Education Publishers), 333–340.

White, Ian (2015) *Environmental Planning in Context* (London: Palgrave).

Wiener, Allen J. (1986) *The Beatles: A Recording History* (Jefferson, NC: McFarland).

Woodside, Arch (2010) *Case Study Research: Theory, Methods and Practice* (Bingley: Emerald).

Wright, Jade (2015) 'The Mathew Street Festival – 40 pictures from a 21 year party' *Liverpool Echo*, 20 August 2015, http://www.liverpoolecho.co.uk/whats-on/mathew-street-festival-40-pictures-9897472 (accessed 7 July 2016).

Zeller, Nancy (1995) 'Narrative strategies for case reports', in *Life History and Narrative*, ed. Amos J. Hatch and Richard Wisniewski (Abingdon: Routledge Falmer), 75–85.

Streaming through a glass onion
Curation, chronology, control and the Beatles' legacy

Steve Jones
University of Illinois Chicago, U.S.A.
sjones@uic.edu

Walter Podrazik
University of Illinois Chicago, U.S.A.
podrazik@ameritech.net

Abstract: This article contextualizes the Beatles' efforts to maintain a consistent chronological narrative of their career, art and achievements in light of commercial and technological advancements in popular music since the 1960s. It examines the tensions between art, authenticity, commerce and chronology to ascertain the contours of fandom, mythmaking and industry that have lent the Beatles the ability to preserve their legacy on their terms. It argues that the Beatles' repeated and consistent efforts to chronologically affirm and fix their narrative allows fans to enter the Beatles' story from multiple points in time and to create their own stories within that chronology, thereby allowing the Beatles to continue to serve as musical and cultural symbols across generations.

Keywords: fandom, mythmaking, authenticity, storytelling, narrative

Introduction

When Paul McCartney returned to touring in May 2022 after two years of Covid hiatus, he added a new historical, multimedia element to his show, projecting footage from the *Get Back* film

The Journal of Beatles Studies Autumn (2022)   ISSN 2754-7019 (online)
https://doi.org/10.3828/jbs.2022.5

of John Lennon singing 'I've Got a Feeling' and sharing vocals once again with his mate. The digital duet between McCartney on stage and Lennon larger-than-life on the screen behind him was an explicit nod to fans who had recently been immersed in the eight-hour *Get Back* film. Among those fans: McCartney himself as both performer and an aficionado of the Beatles.

In addition, this mingling of history, myth and in-the-moment experience was in keeping with more than half a century of efforts by the Beatles to shape their narrative and to shape the fans' experience. During that same time, generations of fans were also crafting their own individual efforts to make their mark on the unfolding story of John Lennon, Paul McCartney, George Harrison and Ringo Starr.

In an essay examining debates about John Lennon's legacy, Janne Mäkela noted that 'the history of the Beatles continues to unfold as a cultural narrative' (Mäkela 2005: 171). Particularly in 2021 as we witnessed the release of the Peter Jackson *The Beatles: Get Back* film and the accompanying round of advance press coverage and interviews, it is clearer than ever that Mäkela was correct. But as the Beatles' music is now available to younger generations via streaming media, and as new Beatles music is issued (and reissued and remixed), what will become of the Beatles' legacy? Does it matter at which point one enters the Beatles' narrative to one's understanding of that legacy, or is their history now so well settled that entry points matter less with regard to their history and more with regard to fans' personal experience? In this article we address these and other questions about the Beatles' legacy as a culturally, generationally, industrially and dynamically constructed narrative that engages audience, music and musicians in an ongoing conversation about the meaning of the music and the band, a conversation that has spanned decades and multiple media, and illustrates the tensions between art and commerce, artist and fan, mythmaking and history in the digital era. The advent of streaming media and its overtaking of physical music formats such as the LP and CD has altered the entry points at which fans not only of the Beatles but of almost any artist first encounter and experience music. As a result artists', and the music industry's, ability to craft a singular narrative has become increasingly complicated during a time in which it may seem as if all elements of the fan experience, not just music, are on 'shuffle mode'.

The day after the music dies

Joli Jensen's concerns, expressed in an essay on Patsy Cline about shifts in image that musicians and celebrities undergo after death, serve as our theoretical foundation. In her essay Jensen asks, 'has something been lost in this "unmooring" from the concrete specificity of the music, and of the life?' (Jensen 2005b: 136). When a musician, or any celebrity, dies, they are discursively unmoored from their creations, no longer able to engage in conversations about them. As Mäkela wrote in Lennon's case, he 'can no longer participate in defining his position and is thus unable to act as a prime authorizer of his stardom' (2005: 174). Yet that dynamic had actually begun to change ten years before Lennon's death, when in the public arena of perception, the Beatles themselves died, as a group. As a result, even as they launched their respective solo careers, the four members were simultaneously reshaping the context of their own ongoing stories within that narrative.

Fans often form strong parasocial relationships with bands and musicians. (For a survey of research on parasocial relationships see Horton and Wohl 1956; Dibble, Harmann and Rosaen 2015; and Tukachinsky, Walter and Saucier 2020.) It should be noted that while most research on parasocial relationships and parasocial interactions focuses on fictional characters and narratives rather than on people, in some ways bands and musicians create essentially fictional personas. In the face of such relationship formation, the break-up of a band, particularly one as popular as the Beatles, necessitates a coming-to-grips-with among fans. As Jones (2005: 5) wrote:

> Who does the work of making sense of the dead? Obviously family and friends of the deceased do. But when it comes to celebrity deaths, many others do as well. Certainly journalists are implicated in the

process of sense-making and mythmaking. Biographers are often involved, too. But fans are part of that process as well. As Richard Schickel points out, in the case of celebrities 'after death, we are finally allowed to take full possession of (their) lives'. (1985: 129)

In the ensuing media, legal and commercial processes that follow a celebrity's death, fans may become more active participants than when the celebrity was alive, perhaps because death permits a retelling and narrativization of the story without interference from the individual at its centre. This has been increasingly true in an era of social media's ascendance (Sanderson and Cheong 2010) as fan discourse has flourished, growing far beyond fests for Beatles fans, fantasy fiction, local meet-up clubs, fanzines, blogs and 'Breakfast with the Beatles' type radio shows to internationally accessible podcasts and the authorized streaming Beatles Channel. But even without all the latest digital tools, an early illustration of the intense fan interest in possessing, narrativizing and shaping the Beatles story came in October 1969 when a handful of ardent fans in the U.S. embraced a bizarre tale — that Paul McCartney had died in 1966 and had been replaced by a lookalike.

These 'Paul is dead' rumours had begun with on-air speculation by a U.S. DJ (Sheffield 2019) as a riff to 'explain' the stylistic differences in the Beatles' music and physical appearance since the *Sgt. Pepper* recordings. The contention: the original Paul was gone. Key to the tale was pointing to alleged secret messages from the rest of the group about McCartney's passing, which only those 'in the know' could catch. Fans embraced this excuse to scan familiar songs and images from albums as part of the task of 'cracking the code'. A dozen years later one fan wrote of intense conversations in the cafeteria of City College of New York in November 1969, when they 'laid on our table ... pictures ... news clippings ... lyrics...' about 'the alleged death of Paul McCartney' (Catone 1982: 138).

The resulting news coverage and chat were entirely audience created, effectively holding on to a Fab Four image just as stories about the group were being eclipsed by their activities as individuals. In fact, the Beatles' group identity was edging into its death throes. This elaborate projection was a precursor to a kind of possessive fan engagement more commonly seen in contemporary times in online communities, social media, etc. (Sanderson and Cheong 2010). Indeed, one wonders to what degree frenzy may have been stirred had there been a medium like the Internet in 1969 with which to spread the rumours.

If we take death first figuratively, to mean the death of the group, and later literally, to mean the murder of John Lennon in 1980 as well as the death of George Harrison in 2001, we see an interesting permutation of the aforementioned sensemaking processes that Jones (2005) identified. In the first instance the band themselves were in the position of making sense of the group's demise, amidst a period during which the demise was not necessarily fully acknowledged by fans or the press, and during which they clashed with one another, sometimes in public, sometimes in court, about the group's future as a commercial, if not necessarily artistic, entity. Nevertheless even during this period the Beatles were (as they and their heirs still are) strongly protective of their history and how their story was told, and by whom. And while there were moments of discord they remained as strongly protective of their story as they were from early on in their career: in his autobiography Brian Epstein trenchantly noted that 'Whatever happens tomorrow, one thing is certain: it must not be allowed to look after itself' (Epstein 1984: 121).

Immediately after news of the break-up in 1970, the public was already recontextualizing that legacy, as were the press and the entertainment industries. The initial 1970s solo albums were not only viewed for competitive chart performance but also scanned for lyrical ripostes by the artists to one another in an unfolding public 'soap opera'. Among those rounds: George Harrison's 'Isn't It a Pity' (*All Things Must Pass* 1970); Paul McCartney's 'Too Many People' (*Ram* 1971); John Lennon's 'How Do You Sleep?' (*Imagine* 1971); Ringo Starr's 'Early 1970' (1971).

The Beatles, meanwhile, kept a tight rein on 'official' retellings of their story, foregoing what were surely numerous offers and opportunities to quickly cash in on their break-up. Lennon initially held back from the public his intended path apart from the group, letting his actions with Yoko Ono speak for themselves before lyrically in 1970 he declared 'the dream is over' ('God', *John Lennon/Plastic Ono Band*). McCartney, meanwhile, in his 'unofficial' announcement of the Beatles' break-up, was deliberately ambiguous. McCartney had told *Life* magazine while responding to the 'Paul is dead' rumours that 'the Beatle thing is over' (Bacon 1969: 105). Yet later, in the staged press release 'interview' circulated with the *McCartney* album (1970) and reprinted in the 2011 *McCartney* Archive edition book, his response to whether this was a rest away from the Beatles or the start of a solo career was 'Time will tell' (McCartney 2011 [1970]: 113).

Yet even in the immediate wake of the break-up Lennon passionately defended the Beatles as the best. In the 'Lennon Remembers' 1970 *Rolling Stone* interviews he pointedly rejected criticism from Mick Jagger: '[Mick] said a lot of sort of tarty things about the Beatles, which I am hurt by, because I can knock the Beatles but don't let Mick Jagger knock them' (Wenner 2002: 66–67). Paul McCartney attended the live ABC Grammy telecast on 16 March 1971 to accept on behalf of the group the composer's award for *Let It Be* (awarded to all of the Beatles) for Original Score, Motion Picture or TV Special (Kaplan 1985: 344). With Linda McCartney at his side, Paul said simply: 'Thank you.'

In the period between then and John Lennon's murder there was always the possibility of some kind of reunion, and the death of the group as such was not seen as final. Even among the former Beatles one could almost sense a hint of reticence in their public comments about declaring with finality that they would not in some manner meet up again. Nor were they above wryly commenting on a reunion themselves, as happened during George Harrison's 1976 appearance on *Saturday Night Live*. The death of John Lennon, of course, put an end to any speculation about a reunion (notwithstanding the 'studio reunion' with Lennon during the course of recording 'Free as a Bird' [1995] and 'Real Love' [1996]), and with the passing of George Harrison the end of the group was reaffirmed.

Lennon's passing saw an outpouring of grief among fans. As Janne Mäkelä wrote, 'Lennon's murder was the catalyst for a new phase that has now lasted longer than the period of his celebrity while he was alive' (2004: 218). Mäkelä goes on to note that 'Such phenomena have ... become more prominent during the age of mechanical and digital reproduction, when the image of a public person can continue to survive and develop without the celebrity being physically present' (218). Since the publication of Mäkelä's 2004 book about Lennon, changes in technology, such as the rise of social media and file sharing, that bring the Beatles' music and images to fans and also provide ways for audiences to engage in unprecedented ways in meaning-making, have altered the industrial and commercial processes by which the band had some degree of control over their legacy. The opportunities to direct the group's legacy from top down are now more difficult than ever. Even the group's musical legacy is challenged: contemporary audio tools allow listeners not only to curate their own Beatles experiences by easily shuffling songs but also to remix them thanks to the availability of individual tracks separated from the band's multi-track recordings that were used for audio in the video game *The Beatles: Rock Band*. The Internet is chock full of Beatles mashups, among the most prominent being *The Grey Album* created by Danger Mouse in 2004 by mixing material from Jay-Z's *The Black Album* with songs from the Beatles' so-called *White Album*. EMI Records made a futile (arguably performative) attempt to block the album, while McCartney was quoted as saying that he didn't mind it, that he felt it was a tribute to the Beatles and that he liked it (Lowe 2005). Before their own archives were collected and curated, the Beatles had found some of the same attraction in early bootlegs as any fan. The unauthorized discs were the opportunity to hear (their own) long-buried moments. According to a WPLJ-FM radio interview, in December 1971 a hustling fan traded a copy of the bootleg disc *Yellow Matter Custard* (then-unreleased BBC tracks) to a curious John Lennon for a Butcher cover sleeve of *Yesterday and Today* (then autographed and dated) (WPLJ 1972). Over time, the Beatles came to recognize the promotional value of creating for and pitching to that ardent collecting audience. McCartney, for example, dubbed an initially limited 1991 release of his musical performance on MTV as *Unplugged (The Official Bootleg)*.

Efforts by historians to determine questions surrounding chronologies, legitimacy and authenticity are made more difficult, too. The proliferation of sources online, and the mortality of those who were there, whether central or peripheral to the Beatles' story, continue to complicate the distillation of truth from myth. These matters are all the more urgent for, as John Kimsey noted in an essay examining *Lennon: His Life and Work* in which he closely looks at the struggles between McCartney and Yoko Ono to control the historical record, 'for anyone interested not just in the Beatles, but in the history and politics of culture itself, the stakes in this struggle are real and rising' (2006: 198). These struggles are now made even more complicated by another 'unmooring', to employ Jensen's evocative term from above, an unmooring set in motion by digital technologies and social media.

Chronology and authenticity

The positioning in time of particular popular music artists, records and even genres has generally been used to mark history in popular music, to denote musical and stylistic origins, and thus the originality or authenticity of music as well. The creation of chrono-logical taxonomies (e.g., *The Complete Rock Family Trees* [Frame 1993]) has been embraced not only by fans but also by musicians.

All four Beatles repeatedly showed their respect and admiration for the definers of R&B and rock & roll and expressed a keen interest in the origins of the music that inspired them. In 1964, they invited Carl Perkins (then on his first tour in Great Britain) to attend their EMI recording session (at which they cut his song 'Matchbox') (Harry 2002). When John Lennon welcomed Chuck Berry to the *Mike Douglas Show* stage in 1972 he declared, 'If you had tried to give rock and roll another name, you might call it Chuck Berry.' At the passing of Little Richard in May 2020, Paul McCartney tweeted: 'Little Richard came screaming into my life when I was a teenager. I owe a lot of what I do to Little Richard and his style; and he knew it. He would say, "I taught Paul everything he knows". I had to admit he was right' (McCartney 2020).

Perhaps the simplest determinant of authenticity is chronology, easily denoted by the date of a record release, or a concert performance. Indeed, particularly in a pre-Internet era, record releases denoted at least a semblance of order (although, as in the case of *Let It Be* and *Abbey Road*, many legal, commercial, and marketing issues could delay a release and alter the chronological order of a recording relative to its availability to the public). If nothing else the copyright dates on record sleeves or labels provided some chronological order. But in the Internet age all music stands alongside other music, readily available at any given moment, largely unaccompanied by text denoting year of copyright, songwriter, publisher or any other textual information of the kind usually found on a record sleeve. The artefact undergoes a form of unmooring not entirely different from the one referenced earlier in Jensen (2005b) but the recording, as Long (2019: 311–312) wrote, nevertheless 'presents us with instances in which the sound of popular music resonates in our hearing, potentially to prompt feelings and reflections on its status as historical artefact in which something, however ineffable, is communicated from and about the past'. Of course, a chronology is still there for those who wish to look it up (most likely now via Wikipedia or Discogs.com), but the timeline has been flattened as more and more music has accumulated and shuffled along with all other music that exists. It is arguable even whether the notion of a 'release' (or 'drop', to put it more contemporaneously) matters to current generations of listeners, but rather only whether or not something is new.

Musical and creative sequencing clearly continue to matter to the Beatles, however. The twenty-first-century expanded anniversary editions of *Sgt. Pepper*, *The Beatles*, *Abbey Road* and *Let It Be* have at their base a sequential narrative grounded in meticulous detail, supported by lengthy essays and the reproduction of historical documents and artefacts. Even after their break-up, the Beatles were and are strictly controlling of the chronology of their music. This was illustrated in early 1973 by the Apple response to the *Alpha Omega* collection, a brazen pirating of already issued Beatles tracks. Successfully sold by mail order and advertised in print and on television in the U.S., the four-disc 59-track unauthorized boxed set arranged a random assortment of group recordings and a few solo tracks in more-or-less alphabetical order (thus the Alpha Omega/'A to Z' title) (Daily Beatle 2020). Apple moved quickly to shut down the release, and also to fill that clearly identified sales gap — a ready audience looking for a generous sampling of the most familiar and popular Beatles music. To that point the group had not yet assembled a greatest hits package spanning their entire career. Rather than a scattershot line-up, this official pair of two-disc sets presented the songs in chronological order in the 'Red' (1962 to 1966) and 'Blue' (1967 to 1970) collections.

Similarly, the *Anthology* television series was entirely chronological in its presentation. The Las Vegas-based Cirque du Soleil *Love* show presents their music in largely chronological order. The timeline is central to their story: the boys meet and befriend one another, go to Hamburg, return to England, the rest is history. And in order to be narrated as history, whether a complete story or one that elides certain details, it must be chronological. Once the group ceases to exist, however, all that remains is history and how it is told. In the case of the Beatles the questions of when the group ceases to exist and who tells its story are interesting ones, complicating matters of chronology, authenticity and legitimacy, debated not only among fans but also in corporate suites and courtrooms and by the group members themselves. Telling and retelling their story chronolog- ically, fixing it in time, was one way the Beatles sought to establish their narrative as the proper one. *The Beatles: Get Back* takes this idea almost to an extreme, using a calendar as an interstitial to move the narrative along. One wonders what the film might have been like had Christopher Nolan been tasked with directing it.[1]

Controlling the past, settling the future

As a matter of historical record, the chronology of the Beatles is most strongly fixed in time twice. The first time was in 1970 when the band broke up and released their last album, *Let It Be*, even though it was recorded before *Abbey Road* which preceded it, to the Beatles' chagrin, further illustrating that the timeline mattered to them. The second time was in 1980 when John Lennon was

1. Or had Jean-Luc Godard been called on to direct *Let It Be*.

murdered. In between, the group members spent most of their time as artists developing solo careers and disengaging from the Beatles, on their own quests to shape their own stories, which have also changed over the decades.

But even early in their career the Beatles (and manager Brian Epstein, it should be noted) were clear in their efforts to establish their timeline and place in history on their own terms. In the 1964 Epstein autobiography, the story is brisk and straightforward, covering Epstein's initial meeting with the group just down the back alley from his record shop and his assuming management, securing a recording contract, guiding their entry onto the world stage and subsequently dealing with ongoing business issues, as they focused on their art.

They defined their celebrity further for public consumption (beyond their record releases) with the faux documentary film *A Hard Day's Night* (1964), continued with the fictional *Help!* (1965) adventure, and they became pure fantasy through the *Yellow Submarine* (1968) feature film (following a light formula cartoon series, *The Beatles*, primarily showcasing their songs, licensed for U.S. television on ABC during the mid-1960s [McNeil 1996]).

By the 1970 release of the *Let It Be* film, though, they were well along with publicly separating from their Beatles identities. No longer performers in their early twenties, their grown-up public images were taking hold. Brian Epstein's death in 1967 left them without his protective intervention, and there was no true successor who carried the credibility of being there from the beginning. Without Epstein they were four individuals with the task of directing themselves, although they were searching for someone to help to fill that role. In *Lennon Remembers* (Wenner 2000: 121), reprinting and expanding in book form the 1970 *Rolling Stone* interviews that helped launch that magazine, John described his efforts at interviewing potential management candidates, leading to his expressed preference for Allen Klein, while Paul was connecting with members of his soon-to-be-wife Linda's family, whose father Lee and brother John Eastman were music business lawyers. Lennon also talks positively about meeting with Klein in the Peter Jackson *Get Back* footage (Day 19).

Unlike the fictional *A Hard Day's Night*, the *Let It Be* film contained actual documentary footage, but with an undefined narrative (apart from writing, rehearsing and recording music) that relied on audiences bringing more information to the film than they received from the movie itself. Gossip, then press report headlines, filled in the gaps. The British *Daily Mirror* posted the bold front-page headline 'Paul is quitting the Beatles' (Short 1970), while the *New York Times* later offered the more restrained 'McCartney breaks off with Beatles' to lead an article by Alvin Shuster on 11 April 1970.

By the time the *Let It Be* movie had its New York premiere on 13 May 1970, the end of the group was treated as a given by reviewers such as Gene Siskel in the Chicago *Tribune*. They regarded the movie's capturing of the Beatles performing together one last time as the chief reason for the wide release of a film otherwise dismissed as 'unimaginative' and 'dull' (Siskel 1970). The documentary nature of the film itself offered little opportunity for countervailing interpretations by fans that this was anything other than the dispirited end of the Beatles, with little room for alternative explanatory narrative.

With *Let It Be*, then, the Beatles and Apple also received a crash course glimpse of losing control of their narrative. The movie required some reading between the cinematic lines as there were half-heard moments and looks exchanged that showed the group adrift. It would take more than half a century for the Peter Jackson-directed *Get Back* to better explore the nuances of that moment. *Get Back* features many more poignant moments that show their loss of control, as when they are marvelling at news stories fabricated from whole cloth or pondering the group's future (perhaps just as fans did not long after the release of the *Let It Be* film). The promotional run-up to the debut of the documentary also clearly illustrated their wish to regain narrative control and establish that period in the band's history as less bad and more productive than it appeared in *Let It Be*.

On the release of *Let It Be* in cinemas, fans had far fewer forums for sharing their thoughts than what has been provided online since the 1990s. Public postings were essentially those from critics whose reviews let their fan sides show apart from cinematic analysis. *Variety* lamented that the Beatles' 'chummy camaraderie' was 'no longer there' and observed that 'Yoko Ono is always present — close at hand, silent, not participating, yet somehow distracting Lennon' (*Variety* 1970: 26). Today we can imagine online forums flooded with questions such as: What happened? Was it the presence of Yoko Ono? Paul McCartney's take-charge self-promotion? George Harrison's unhappiness at being too often ignored, especially seen in the light of his strong showing on the already released out-of-chronological-order *Abbey Road* (with 'Here Comes the Sun' and 'Something' among the strongest tracks)? Or was it just time to move on? Live solo concerts by John Lennon (begun in 1969), George Harrison (in 1971), and Paul McCartney (in 1972) supported an affirmative response to the latter, but the speed and scale of fan discourse and artist pronouncements extended the duration of mystery and myth.

Another marker took place on the *Billboard* magazine charts which on 12 June 1971 ended 385 consecutive weeks in which there had been at least one Beatles title on the publication's Top 200 albums list. That continuous group presence had extended back to 1 February 1964 (Castleman and Podrazik 1976: 357–365).

For an additional 71 weeks there was at least one solo album on the top 200 chart, but there were no further appearances of Beatles albums. Fan expectations shifted from awaiting the next Beatles album as a matter of course to speculating whether the group would ever 'get back together', while also scouring credits to see whether any had worked on another's solo album.

A new era of chart placements began on 14 April 1973 as the Beatles returned, but not with new material. Instead, it was a celebration of the past with a pair of authorized greatest hits packages (with track selection primarily supervised by George Harrison) (Doggett 2009: 203). While those were quickly followed by solo releases from each of the four, beginning in May with albums by Paul McCartney (*Red Rose Speedway*) and George Harrison (*Living in the Material World*), and in November by Ringo Starr (*Ringo*) and John Lennon (*Mind Games*), the two Beatles greatest hits packages continued a seventy-week run on the U.S. charts (Castleman and Podrazik 1976: 364–365).

The four were all still part of the EMI/Capitol contract and, in fact, the greatest hits packages even included a summary listing insert of all the releases, group and solo, to that point. The Beatles canon held treasured memories even as the four pursued their individual careers.

In spring 1974 one enthusiastic fan, Mark Lapidos, looking to commemorate the tenth anniversary of the group's arrival in the U.S., successfully approached John Lennon and essentially asked for his blessing on holding a fan festival. As Lapidos recounts on his website: 'John's response was simple: "I'm all for it. I'm a Beatles Fan too!"' (Lapidos 2014). Buoyed by Lennon's thumbs-up, Lapidos planned and staged his first 'Fest' in New York City that September, drawing some 8000 attendees.[2] All four Beatles donated musical instruments to be auctioned for charity. *Rolling Stone* featured the event in a cover story, 'Strange rumblings in Pepperland' (Siegel 1974).

In 1976, however, there was a far more significant change in the Beatles narrative. That year marked the expiration of their nine-year EMI contract. At that point, there was no new contract, and the Beatles/Apple could see the results of business decisions by EMI and Capitol in both the U.S. and U.K. The two companies conceived and promoted Beatles material to fill their 'Beatles product pipelines' rather than reflecting the preferences of the group members themselves.

Without group input, previously released tracks were treated as fair game for repackaging. There were multiple thematic albums including the U.S. packages *Rock'n'Roll Music* (1976), *Love Songs* (1977) and *Reel Music* (1982, music from their movies), as well as the U.K. *Ballads* (1980) (Castleman and Podrazik 1985). All of these picked apart the carefully conceived original contents of the records as Capitol and EMI skimmed through the Beatles catalogue, plucking songs by type to fit each album umbrella. Critic Nicholas Schaffner (author of *The Beatles Forever*) dismissed the *Rock'n'Roll Music* collection as 'shoddy' and 'tacky' — bolstering the point by citing Ringo Starr's criticisms at the time

2. The Fest for Beatles Fans was originally called Beatlefest.

in *Rolling Stone* and *Melody Maker* where he had fumed, 'All of us looked at the cover of *Rock 'n' Roll Music* and we could hardly bear to see it.' And 'It made us look cheap and we were never cheap' (Schaffner 1978: 188). Additional singles were pulled from existing albums, most successfully in 1976 with Top 10 placement for both 'Got to Get You into My Life' (U.S.) and 'Yesterday' as a single release for the first time in the U.K. Even with their chart and sales success, both singles reflected EMI/Capitol priorities, not those of the Beatles. Although McCartney was on his first U.S. tour at the time in 1976, he did not alter his stage show to incorporate 'Got to Get You into My Life' even though it was then his latest (Beatles) hit. Its release was someone else's plan, not his. In Great Britain, the problem with the 'Yesterday' single was more nuanced. In 1965, issuing 'Yesterday' as a single had been a U.S. endeavour and it became the most successful of all Beatles songs. The problem was the U.K. B-side, 'Twist and Shout', which departed from the approach taken by every other official Beatles single issued in the U.K. to that point in that it was not an original group composition.

The Beatles had seen such record company treatment with one of their heroes, Buddy Holly, following his death in 1958. In that case, familiar tracks were repackaged. In addition, previously unreleased material was issued, including demos and alternate takes, often enhanced by overdubbing by other musicians. In Great Britain, a steady stream of 'new' Buddy Holly releases continued into the mid-1960s, with several singles reaching the U.K. Top 20 ('Reminiscing', 'Brown-Eyed Handsome Man' and 'Bo Diddley'), as cited in the *Guinness World Records British Hit Singles Volume 14* (Roberts 2001).[3] Paul McCartney said in the third episode of *McCartney 3, 2, 1* (2021) that the Beatles had been encouraged to take a similar approach to packaging and repackaging their recordings, but they declined such advice 'because we were recently record buyers and we would have felt so cheated if we'd have bought that (kind of) record'.

3. 'Reminiscing' #17 (chart entry 13 September 1962); 'Brown-Eyed Handsome Man' #3 (chart entry 14 March 1963); 'Bo Diddley' #4 (chart entry 6 June 1963).

Such a fan connection to the music was reflected in Paul McCartney's decision to invest in music publishing outside his own work. One of his first ventures was his 1973 acquisition of the Buddy Holly catalogue. That not only brought a personal lifelong favourite into his own business portfolio, but it also gave him the opportunity to provide a fan's appreciation for the work. Beginning in 1976, McCartney spearheaded in Great Britain an annual Buddy Holly Week celebration, whose events ranged from simple anniversary media displays and catalogue promotions to occasional special concerts and performance events (White 1980; The Paul McCartney Project 2021).

McCartney's respectful curation of Buddy Holly's legacy stood in contrast to the immediate excess of releases from the Beatles catalogue in the mid-1970s. Yet by the end of the decade a more disciplined approach emerged for Beatles material going into the 1980s. All concerned recognized that John Lennon, Paul McCartney, George Harrison and Ringo Starr would continue to develop as solo artists, disengaged from the Beatles, shaping their own stories. At the same time, they recognized that the period from 1962 to 1970 was their defining calling card and leveraged that starting point repeatedly. As an example, not long after the Beatles broke up, when Lennon appeared with Yoko Ono on the *Dick Cavett* TV show (aired on 11 September 1971) promoting his latest solo ventures, he used the question of whether Ono was 'the lady who brought the Beatles apart' to fashion his narrative line. This was part of an ongoing continuum. Respecting the Beatles, but also moving on, Lennon countered with: 'If she took them apart then please give her credit for all the nice music that George made and Ringo made and Paul made and I made since they broke up.' And in more contemporary times, Paul McCartney's 2021 *Lyrics* collection, while drawing from throughout his career, uses as its foundation the Beatles years. The songs are arranged alphabetically, not chronologically, but for the general public there is no mistaking the draw: the Beatles years. In that context, McCartney offers his (latest) take on the story throughout the book. George Harrison's collections of song lyrics, *I Me Mine*, did the same (Harrison 1980; 2017). Ringo Starr's 2022 photo book *Lifted* is similarly Beatles-forward (Starr 2022).

Even more important for shaping their legacy, Apple quietly pursued policies that would, over several decades, serve to 'correct' the preserved recorded history of the group in its biggest market, the United States. At every opportunity, Apple moved to replace albums that had been uniquely assembled for the U.S. market, putting in their place the official collections that had been issued in England. This began in 1978 by making both the U.S. and the U.K. versions of albums available in the U.S. market with a boxed set of all the British releases officially issued for the first time as *The Beatles Collection* (Castleman and Podrazik 1985: 34–50). The introduction of CDs helped to accelerate these efforts, with Beatles material held back from the CD format until 1986. When the discs were issued, the original British packaging and track order were used worldwide, and that is what new generations discovering the Beatles on CD found. There were no official releases of the U.S. configurations until after the British line-ups were well established and those U.S. albums were at last offered as CDs decades later as collectible novelties.

Each new platform offered the Beatles and Apple opportunities to further solidify not only ownership and control, but also the quality of the Beatles catalogue. Tessler (2014: 60) noted perceptively that by the late 1970s the Beatles were 'regularly speaking out against grey market uses of their songs, recordings and other trademarked assets while simultaneously developing their own plans for exploitation'. The authorized use of Beatles music for the *Rock Band* video game provided budgetary support that allowed preparation not only for that project but also for future audio releases. Such efforts were handled by Giles Martin, son of Beatles producer George Martin, and therefore kept 'within the family', so to speak, and not outsourced to engineers and producers not already affiliated with the Beatles.

Other projects with separate revenue streams similarly benefited the recorded material under the control of Apple, on behalf of the Beatles. These included the tracks for the Cirque du Soleil *Love* stage show in Las Vegas, digital remastering of the *Yellow Submarine Songtrack* for a 1999 reissue of the *Yellow Submarine* feature film (Spizer 2003: 288), and the Ron Howard Beatles touring film *Eight*

Days a Week. Maxim Tvorun-Dunn makes a convincing case that the Beatles can be understood as early progenitors of transmedia convergence, 'in which each text (single, album, live performance, film, etc.) acts as a singular node, such as among a web' (2022: 7). Rather as they did in self-referential compositions such as 'Glass Onion', the Beatles could spin complicated webs indeed both in their art as well as in their business ventures, but they put the band at the centre of them all.

Authenticity and authority

After 1980, once it was clear that there could never be a Beatles reunion, the focus permanently shifted. Individual scripting of Beatles events became more than different perspectives by the four players who were there, each emphasizing the story as they saw it. Paul McCartney explained in a 2015 *Esquire* interview that, once past the horror of the act, when John was shot he became 'a martyr. A JFK.' The act 'elevated him to a James Dean'. That in turn led to what McCartney saw as 'a love of revisionism' — most striking the assumption that John Lennon *was* the Beatles (Bilmes 2015).

Joli Jensen, in an essay on fandom, celebrity, mediation and death, wrote:

> What happens when we remember our famous musical dead? There are clearly constraints on the process — commercial as well as symbolic constraints. Posthumous celebrity is an interaction between these constraints that also enacts possibilities. During the payola scandals, Dick Clark famously said that no amount of airplay could 'turn a stiff into a hit'. What he disingenuously ignored is that, nonetheless, airplay is required for all hits to become hits. Commercial processes are what make posthumous celebrity possible, what give fans, journalists, critics, and scholars the materials we use to tell ourselves stories. (2005a: xx)

While the Beatles, and their heirs, have in the sixty years since the group emerged on the world stage been crafting their story, so, too, have fans, aided and abetted by the very same industrial processes the group uses to reach its audience. And while new technologies and new platforms, from the early days of the Internet and chat groups, to the Web, social media, and streaming media, have afforded the Beatles and Apple opportunities to extend their reach and tell their story as they see it and wish it to be seen, they have also afforded opportunities for fans to engage in their own storytelling and mythmaking. Indeed, it is striking how necessarily symbiotic the relationship is between the Beatles and their fans, how dependent chronicling the group's story is on someone else doing the transcribing/theorizing. Even while annotating the eight hours of *Get Back*, day-by-day (as on BeatlesBible.com), among fans there are also developing narratives exploring what else was going on off-screen in that period. Not part of the official story, not musical, not on film, but secondary information gleaned by mining elsewhere. Past memoirs such as Pattie Boyd's *Wonderful Tonight* (2007) offer speculative fodder as to why George was in a sour milk sea mood in early January when splitting from the group. Trouble at home? A cheating affair? Boyd's telling comments: 'I couldn't stand it so I went to London' and 'Six days later George phoned me to say that the girl had gone and I went home' (2007: 123). In short, no matter how 'official' an effort *Get Back* may have been, others continue to further shape the story, and, thanks to the instantaneity of the Internet, were able to do so in real time at the documentary's debut.

The passing of time, of course, matters, too. Only McCartney and Starr are still alive, and fewer and fewer people can claim to have 'been there' at various moments in Beatles history. What might happen when none of the four Beatles remain to tell their story? Technology is already moving past the techniques Peter Jackson used to restore footage for *Get Back*, as was made clear by the 'appearance' of Tupac Shakur at the Coachella music festival in 2012, and the ABBA avatars 'reunion' in 2021. Surely the Beatles and Apple have already been approached with offers to 'preserve' them in some virtual form. There are additional questions regarding who will have control of the Beatles' commercial endeavours. How long will their estates (or they themselves) remain impervious to the kinds of offers for catalogues paid to musicians such as Dylan and Springsteen, for instance?

Technologies that rely on algorithms for personalization and curation are also altering the ability of any individual entity, whether a person or corporation, to effectively control curation. The affective investments fans make in popular music and musicians are themselves altered by the media through which the connections with and relationships to them are made (Jones 2011). Streaming media have all but supplanted almost all media that had come before them and in turn have become the primary means by which people, particularly young people, listen to music. The focus of official releases now seems to be on adding value by including books, posters, outtakes, etc.,[4] in deluxe packaging, thus providing something that streaming cannot (and, in some cases, capitalizing on the resurgence of interest in vinyl records as a tangible artefact by contrast to digital media). What is important to remember is that the mediation between artist and fan is 'bidirectional', as Tofalvy noted, and that 'Who is being represented as authentic in the relevant taste community — in other words, how successfully they accumulate their cultural capital — is dependent partly on how the available musical stocks are stored and displayed' (2020: 12). Similarly, the formats chosen by artists and record companies communicate to fans about the value and authenticity of the material they enclose. That most music consumption now takes place via streaming audio disrupts (to admittedly use an overused term) this bidirectional flow, and the Beatles and Apple seem to be getting in their last licks at establishing a more material relationship with fans with numerous official deluxe reissues and releases in the 2010s and 2020s. It will be interesting to see whether such efforts find new fans coming into the fold or are offerings that only existing fans are taking up.

But the most interesting issues might arise when Paul and Ringo pass away. What will be the response of fans? When Lennon died the Internet as we know it now did not exist. When Harrison died in 2001 it was still nascent: MySpace launched in 2003 and Facebook in 2004. The instant online connection among millions of fans

---

4. Even including tchotchkes like garden gnomes, in the case of George Harrison's *All Things Must Pass* deluxe reissue.

simultaneously may result in an unprecedented memorializing. But will it be memorializing the Beatles, the group, or the individual members? Has the forty-plus years since Lennon's death and the fifty-plus years since the group's break-up provided sufficient time for grieving the group's demise, enough such that, by contrast with more recent musicians' deaths (*e.g.*, Tom Petty, Meat Loaf, John Prine, Little Richard, to name a few) remembrance will be muted?

Furthermore, what will memorial efforts mean? As Andsager noted about websites intended to memorialize musicians no longer living, 'The fans who post their thoughts on webshrines are particularly aware of the need to regenerate celebrity. Both fans and webshriners employ superlatives to describe their feelings for the celebrities, many of which suggest that the deceased are now larger than life' (2005: 26). The Beatles have been 'larger than life' for decades. It will be interesting to see how much larger fans will attempt to make them, or whether the mythmaking that ensues will result in renewed storytelling about the Beatles. Jensen noted that 'mourning dead celebrities ... [is] an interpretive process that enriches, deepens and makes life more meaningful for all concerned ... [and] is a more creative and complex cultural conversation than ever before' (2005a: xxii). The ability to share not only words and feelings but also, via new media, expression by way of playlists, as on Spotify, or movement and dances, as on TikTok, for example, will undoubtedly foster new forms of memorialization and sharing of grief and celebration.

By the 2020s McCartney and Starr, and to an extent Lennon and Harrison's estates, had established strong measures for preserving and continuing the legacy of the Beatles, through Apple. The greatest asset they reclaimed was coordinating control of the group's actual recordings. Universal obtained ownership when the company bought most of EMI in 2011 (Perpetua 2011), thereafter using a wholly owned subsidiary, Calderstone Productions Limited, for the new products (Beatles Blogger 2014). They repeatedly refreshed the material to contemporary technical standards when both technology and commercial opportunity allowed. These recordings introduced the Beatles to new generations of listeners, while providing fresh infusions of capital to Apple. They effectively leveraged this proven content through multiple delivery forms, from radio and records to digital and beyond.

And by the 2020s, music publishing for the Lennon–McCartney songbook was in firm hands, split between Sony and Paul McCartney. Over the years McCartney had systematically taken advantage of opportunities in U.S. copyright law to reclaim his portion of the co-authored Beatles songs, building from the beginning. Sony had acquired a portion of publishing rights through a separate arrangement with Yoko Ono (as widow-owner of John Lennon's share), along with ownership of rights purchased, then surrendered, by Michael Jackson. Licensing not only generated its own revenue stream, it also provided leverage over those seeking to use this material for any project, any storytelling – and a powerful tool against unauthorized exploitation.

These controls have served as the building blocks for one of the most potent aspects of the Beatles legacy through narrative, music and visuals. New media, however, have whittled away at their control of those blocks. Apple has guarded and curated its official story of John, Paul, George and Ringo, and over time allowed that it is not spotless, while compartmentalizing any excesses so as not to detract from the promotable legend of the working-class kids who made good,[5] as musical geniuses at work.

Conclusion: preserving the legacy

Guarding music and visuals in the digital domain is difficult, and perhaps impossible. The digital age has allowed new generations of fans, even without an actual instrument in hand, to immerse themselves in Beatles music at their computers and screens, to play along, manipulate tracks and layer themselves into the mix – in

5. The eight hours of the Peter Jackson *The Beatles: Get Back* documentary perfectly reflected this approach. This was a reality show ride through the Beatles' creative process, over-the-shoulder access guaranteed to delight any fan, with unrehearsed footage and frank dialogue. Yet even that still left most of the month of January 1969 unfilmed, and much of what was filmed unshared.

the process potentially forming a deep musical bond cutting across generations and eras. There is every probability that a generation of fans not only discovered the Beatles through the *Rock Band* video game but that they also maintain a deep fondness for the group by virtue of its multi-user game play, for instance, that brought friends and families together in front of the screen.

All of these elements have given the Beatles through Apple and its partners the type of artistic control and, importantly, longevity that would have pleased manager Brian Epstein. Back in 1962, on the rejection of the group by Decca records, Epstein had declared that 'one day they will be bigger than Elvis Presley' (Epstein 1984: 55). Six decades later it is clear that that was too low a bar. At this point in the canons of music, the Beatles can be offered as artists on a par with their contemporaries across musical genres, from Stephen Sondheim to the Rolling Stones.

It is worth noting, however, that no artist's career trajectory is constantly upward, or even steady. As Eamonn Forde reminds us, quoting EMI's Tony Wadsworth, 'We always think of the Beatles as being this always-massive catalogue which stays at a certain level but it ebbed and flowed' (Forde 2021: 146).[6] Wadsworth's comment was in reference to the resurgence of interest in the Beatles brought about by the rise of Oasis and reiterates the notion that storytelling and chronology matter: which Beatles — the Hamburg, moptop, psychedelic or rooftop ones — would be most easily associated with Oasis? If EMI and Apple were to capitalize on this, which entry point, from a marketing standpoint, would be most sensible to use to attract new fans? Another reason chronology matters is that in the absence of obvious entry points such as that provided by Oasis/Britpop, and in an era when fans may encounter the Beatles of any era[7] (potentially side by side) it is easiest to tell

6. Forde also does a deep dive into the Beatles' and their heirs' direction of Apple and its relationship with EMI in a chapter assaying EMI's tensions with its biggest acts as the record company foundered (Forde 2019: 143–161).

7. It is worth noting that few bands have gone through the transformations the Beatles did, and in so short a period of time. That we can note 'eras' in their career is itself rather remarkable.

the Beatles' story chronologically, as with the *Anthology* television series, and rely on the overall arc of that story to be sufficiently compelling to old and new fans alike.

To that end, in the case of the Beatles, the lines between art and commerce, myth and history, and fan and artist have long been irreversibly blurred. It is our contention, returning to Jensen's notion that stars are 'unmoored' when they die, that the Beatles were never entirely 'moored' symbolically in the first place, and that their efforts to control their story over *and with* time gave them the singular opportunity to represent themselves as 'the Beatles'. The multiple meanings ascribed to 'the Beatles' are largely dependent on both when one encounters them (that is, at what age and in which circumstances) as well as in which period (lovable moptops, psychedelic musicians, rooftop performers, etc.). As a consequence, the Beatles' legacy has the potential to endure as a cultural narrative to be embraced by new-found fans across the centuries precisely because the Beatles have insistently engaged in long-term efforts to perpetuate their own narrative as fixed in time. Even as the affordances of new media focus less on chronology and more on affect and engagement with audiences, the Beatles' own storytelling has afforded fans easy temporal hooks on which to hang their own Beatles stories.

Going forward, that Beatles narrative will endure as audiences continue telling our stories to one another, finding ourselves within their and our chronologies, adding individuals' narratives to the official chronology, mingling history and myth, the personal with the musical and the commercial.

Bibliography

Andsager, Julie (2005) 'Altared sites: celebrity webshrines as shared mourning', in *Afterlife as Afterimage: Understanding Posthumous Fame*, ed. Steve Jones and Joli Jensen (New York: Peter Lang), 17–30.

Bacon, Dorothy (1969) 'The case of the missing Beatle — Paul is still with us', *Life*, 7 November 1969: 105.

Beatles Blogger (2014) 'The Beatles and Calderstone Productions
    Limited', Beatles Blog, 9 February 2014, https://beatlesblogger.
    com/2014/02/09/the-beatles-and-calderstone-productions-limited/
    (accessed 28 February 2022).
Bilmes, Alexis (2015) 'Paul McCartney is *Esquire*'s August cover star',
    Esquire Magazine, 7 February 2015, https://www.esquire.com/
    uk/culture/news/a8511/paul-mccartney-interview/ (accessed
    22 February 2022).
Boyd, Pattie with Penny Junor (2007) *Wonderful Tonight — George
    Harrison, Eric Clapton, and Me* (New York: Harmony Books).
Castleman, Harry and Walter Podrazik (1976) *All Together Now: The First
    Complete Beatles Discography* (Ann Arbor, MI: Pierian Press).
Castleman, Harry and Walter Podrazik (1985) *The End of The Beatles?*
    (Ann Arbor, MI: Pierian Press).
Catone, Marc A. (1982) *As I Write This Letter: An American Generation
    Remembers The Beatles* (Ann Arbor, MI: Greenfield Books/Pierian
    Press).
The Daily Beatle (2020) 'The Beatles: Alpha Omega', 19 March 2015
    (updated 29 June 2020), http://webgrafikk.com/blog/uncate-
    gorized/the-beatles-alpha-omega/ (accessed 22 February 2022).
Dibble, Jayson L., Tilo Hartmann and Sarah F. Rosaen (2015) 'Parasocial
    interaction and parasocial relationship: conceptual clarification
    and a critical assessment of measures', *Human Communication
    Research* 42: 21–44.
Doggett, Peter (2009) *You Never Give Me Your Money: The Battle for the
    Soul of The Beatles* (London: Bodley Head).
Epstein, Brian (1984) *A Cellarful of Noise,* repr. edn with additions (Ann
    Arbor, MI: Pierian Press).
Forde, Eamonn (2019) *The Final Days of EMI: Selling the Pig* (London:
    Omnibus Press).
Forde, Eamonn (2021) *Leaving the Building: The Lucrative Afterlife of
    Music Estates* (London: Omnibus Press).
Frame, Pete (1993) *The Complete Rock Family Trees* (New York: Omnibus
    Press).
Harrison, George (1980) *I Me Mine* (New York: Simon and Schuster).
Harrison, George (2017) *I Me Mine — Extended Edition* (Guildford: Genesis
    House).
Harry, Bill (2002) 'The Beatles and Carl Perkins', Mersey Beat [website],
    http://www.triumphpc.com/mersey-beat/beatles/beatlesandcarlp-
    erkins.shtml (accessed 22 February 2022).

Horton, Donald and R. Richard Wohl (1956) 'Mass communication and para-social interaction: observations on intimacy at a distance', *Psychiatry* 19: 215–229.

Jensen, Joli (2005a) 'Introduction – on fandom, celebrity, and mediation: posthumous possibilities', in *Afterlife as Afterimage: Understanding Posthumous Fame*, ed. Steve Jones and Joli Jensen (New York: Peter Lang), xv–xxiii.

Jensen, Joli (2005b) 'Posthumous Patsy Clines: constructions of identity in hillbilly heaven', in *Afterlife as Afterimage: Understanding Posthumous Fame*, ed. Steve Jones and Joli Jensen (New York: Peter Lang), 121–141.

Jones, Steve (2005) 'Better off dead: or, making it the hard way', in *Afterlife as Afterimage: Understanding Posthumous Fame*, ed. Steve Jones and Joli Jensen (New York: Peter Lang), 3–16.

Jones, Steve (2011) 'Music and the Internet', in *The Handbook of Internet Studies*, ed. Mia Conslavo and Charles Ess (Oxford: Wiley-Blackwell), 440–451.

Kaplan, Mike (ed.) (1985) *Variety Presents the Complete Book of Major U.S. Show Business Awards* (New York: Garland Publishing).

Kimsey, John (2006) 'Spinning the historical record: Lennon, McCartney, and museum politics', in *Reading the Beatles: Cultural Studies, Literary Criticism, and the Fab Four*, ed. Kenneth Womack and Todd F. Davis (Albany, NY: State University of New York Press), 197–213.

Lapidos, Mark (2014) 'How the Fest was born...', The Fest for Beatles Fans [website], https://www.thefest.com/history/#.YhLAY5ZMHD4 (accessed 22 February 2022).

Long, Paul (2019) 'The poetics of recorded time: listening again to popular music history', *Popular Music History* 12(3): 295–315.

Lowe, Zane and Paul McCartney (2005) 'Paul McCartney talks Jay-Z, Danger Mouse, 99 Problems v Helter Skelter' [clip of radio broadcast], broadcast 12 September 2005 on BBC Radio 1, uploaded to YouTube by ClarkKent768 on 29 May 2021, https://www.youtube.com/watch?v=nbO2xqwvmG8 (accessed 18 February 2022).

Mäkelä, Janne (2004) *John Lennon Imagined: Cultural History of a Rock Star* (New York: Peter Lang).

Mäkela, Janne (2005) 'Who owns him? The debate on John Lennon', in *Afterlife as Afterimage: Understanding Posthumous Fame*, ed. Steve Jones and Joli Jensen (New York: Peter Lang), 171–190.

McCartney, Paul (2011 [1970]) *McCartney* [album book], The Paul McCartney Archive Collection (Beverly Hills: MPL Communications).

McCartney, Paul (2020) Twitter post, 6:15 AM, 10 May 2020, https://twitter.com/PaulMcCartney/status/1259441969304133632 (accessed 18 February 2022).

McCartney, Paul (2021) *The Lyrics: 1956 to the Present*, 2 vols, ed. Paul Muldoon (New York: Liveright Publishing).

The Paul McCartney Project (2021) 'Paul McCartney acquires Buddy Holly's song catalog', https://www.the-paulmccartney-project.com/1973/02/paul-mccartney-acquires-buddy-hollys-song-catalog/ (accessed 20 May 2022).

McNeil, Alex (1996) 'The Beatles Cartoon Series', in *Total Television,* 4th edn (New York: Penguin Books), 82.

Perpetua, Matthew (2011) 'Universal Music Group purchases EMI Music', *Rolling Stone,* 11 November 2011, https://www.rollingstone.com/music/music-news/universal-music-group-purchases-emi-music-233091/ (accessed 22 February 2022).

Roberts, David (ed.) (2001) *Guinness World Records British Hit Singles,* 14th edn (Guinness World Records Publishing).

Sanderson, Jimmy and Pauline Hope Cheong (2010) 'Tweeting prayers and communicating grief over Michael Jackson online', *Bulletin of Science, Technology & Society* 30(5): 328–340.

Schaffner, Nicholas (1978) *The Beatles Forever* (New York: McGraw-Hill).

Schickel, Richard (1985) *Intimate Strangers: The Culture of Celebrity* (Garden City, NY: Doubleday).

Sheffield, Rob (2019) 'Paul is dead: the bizarre story of music's most notorious conspiracy theory', *Rolling Stone,* 11 October 2019, https://www.rollingstone.com/music/music-features/paul-mccartney-is-dead-conspiracy-897189/ (accessed 22 February 2022).

Short, Don (1970) 'Paul is quitting the Beatles', *Daily Mirror* [London], 10 April 1970: 1.

Shuster, Alvin (1970) 'McCartney breaks off with Beatles', *New York Times,* 11 April 1970: 20.

Siegel, Joel (1974) 'Strange rumblings in Pepperland', *Rolling Stone,* 24 October 1974.

Siskel, Gene (1970) 'Let It Be' [review], *Chicago Tribune,* 25 May 1970.

Spizer, Bruce (2003) *The Beatles on Apple Records* (New Orleans: 498 Productions).

Starr, Ringo (2022) *Lifted* (Nottingham: Julien's Auctions PlusArt Ltd).

Tessler, Holly (2014) 'Let it be? Exploring the Beatles grey market, 1970–1995', *Popular Music History* 9(1): 48–63.

Tofalvy, Tamas (2020) 'Continuity and change in the relationship between popular music, culture, and technology: an introduction', in *Popular Music, Technology, and the Changing Media Ecosystem,* ed. Tamas Tofalvy and Emilia Barna (Cham: Palgrave MacMillan), 1–22.

Tukachinsky, Riva, Nathan Walter and Camille J. Saucier (2020) 'Antecedents and effects of parasocial relationships: a meta-analysis', *Journal of Communication* 70: 868–894.

Tvorun-Dunn, Maxim (2022) '"I am he as you are he as you are me and we are all together": transmedia convergence of the Beatles' psychedelic years (1966–1969)', *Popular Music History* 14(3): 1–21.

Variety (1970) 'Let It Be' [film review], 20 May 1970: 15, 26.

Wenner, Jann S. (2000) *Lennon Remembers,* new edn (London: Verso).

White, Chris (1980) 'Buddy's Week 1976–80', *Music Week/Club Sandwich Supplement,* September 1980: 10.

WPLJ-FM (1972) 'John Lennon's reaction to an early Beatles Bootleg LP: Yellow Matter Custard', broadcast 23 January 1972 and uploaded to YouTube by spinalcrackerbox 8 March 2013, https://www.youtube.com/watch?v=qg2Fxnkz1Ac (accessed 21 May 2022).

Discography

The Beatles, 'Here Comes the Sun', *Abbey Road.* Apple. 1969.

The Beatles, 'Something', *Abbey Road.* Apple. 1969.

The Beatles, *Abbey Road.* Apple. 1969.

The Beatles, 'Free As A Bird', *Anthology 1.* Apple. 1995.

The Beatles, 'Real Love', *Anthology 2.* Apple. 1996.

The Beatles, *The Beatles* [also *White Album*]. Apple. 1968.

The Beatles, *The Beatles 1962 to 1966* ['Red Album']. Apple. 1973.

The Beatles, *The Beatles 1967 to 1970* ['Blue Album']. Apple. 1973.

The Beatles, *The Beatles Ballads.* Parlophone. 1980.

The Beatles, *The Beatles Collection* [box set]. Capitol. Parlophone. Apple. 1978.

The Beatles, 'Got to Get You into My Life' [single]. Capitol. 1976.

The Beatles, *Let It Be.* Apple. 1970.

The Beatles, 'Matchbox', *Long Tall Sally* [EP]. Parlophone. 1964.

The Beatles, *Love (Soundtrack remix).* Apple. 2006.

The Beatles, *Love Songs.* Capitol. Parlophone. 1977.

The Beatles, *Reel Music*. Capitol. Parlophone. 1982.
The Beatles, *Rock 'n' Roll Music*. Capitol. Parlophone. 1976.
The Beatles, *Yellow Matter Custard* [bootleg album]. Multiple
    unauthorized labels. 1971.
The Beatles, *Yellow Submarine Songtrack*. Apple. 1999.
The Beatles, 'Yesterday' b/w 'Twist and Shout' [single]. Parlophone.
    1976.
Buddy Holly, 'Bo Diddley', *Reminiscing*. Coral Records. 1963.
Buddy Holly, 'Brown-Eyed Handsome Man', *Reminiscing*. Coral Records.
    1963.
Buddy Holly, 'Reminiscing', *Reminiscing*. Coral Records. 1963.
Danger Mouse, *The Grey Album*. [No label.] 2004.
George Harrison, 'Isn't It a Pity', *All Things Must Pass*. Apple. 1970.
George Harrison, *Living in the Material World*. Apple. 1973.
Jay-Z, *The Black Album*. Rock-a-Fella Def Jam. 2003.
John Lennon, 'God', *John Lennon/Plastic Ono Band*. Apple. 1970.
John Lennon, 'How Do You Sleep?', *Imagine*. Apple. 1971.
John Lennon, *Mind Games*. Apple. 1973.
Paul McCartney, *McCartney*. Apple. 1970.
Paul McCartney, *Unplugged (The Official Bootleg)*. Parlophone. 1991.
Paul and Linda McCartney, 'Too Many People', *Ram*. Apple. 1971.
Paul McCartney and Wings, *Red Rose Speedway*. Apple. 1973.
Ringo Starr, 'Early 1970' [single]. Apple. 1971.
Ringo Starr, *Ringo*. Apple. 1973.

Filmography

Brodax, Al (producer) (1965–1969) *The Beatles* [cartoon series], ABC
    Television.
Dunning, George (dir.) (1968) *Yellow Submarine*.
Harrison, George (performer) (1976) *Saturday Night Live*, hosted by Paul
    Simon, produced by Lorne Michaels, NBC Television, 20 November
    1976.
Heinzerling, Zachary (dir.) (2021) *McCartney 3, 2, 1* [mini-series], Hulu.
Howard, Ron (dir.) (2016) *The Beatles: Eight Days A Week — The Touring
    Years*.
Jackson, Peter (dir.) (2021) *The Beatles: Get Back*.
Lennon, John and Chuck Berry (performers) (1972) *The Mike Douglas
    Show*, syndicated, 15 February 1972.

Lennon, John and Yoko Ono (performers) (1971) *The Dick Cavett Show*, ABC Television, 11 September 1971.

Lester, Richard (dir.) (1964) *A Hard Day's Night*.

Lester, Richard (dir.) (1965) *Help!*

Lindsay-Hogg, Michael (dir.) (1970) *Let It Be.*

McCartney, Paul (performer) (1971) 'GRAMMY Rewind: Paul McCartney Accepts the GRAMMY for Best Original Score at the 1971 GRAMMYs' [broadcast on ABC Television 16 March 1971], Grammy.com, https://www.grammy.com/videos/paul-mccartney-accepts-grammy-best-original-score-1971-grammys-grammy-rewind (accessed 22 February 2022).

Wonfor, Geoff (dir.) (1995) *The Beatles Anthology* [television series], ITV and ABC Television.

Beatlemania

On informational cascades and spectacular success

Cass R. Sunstein
Robert Walmsley University Professor,
Harvard University, U.S.A.
Areeda Hall 225, Harvard Law School, Cambridge, MA 02138
csunstei@law.harvard.edu

Abstract: Why did the Beatles become a worldwide sensation? Why do some cultural products succeed, and others fail? On one view, the simplest and most general explanation is best, and it points to quality, appropriately measured: the Beatles succeeded because of the sheer quality of their music. On another view, timely enthusiasm or timely indifference can make the difference for all, including the Beatles, and informational cascades are often necessary for spectacular success. For those who emphasize informational cascades, success and failure are not inevitable; they depend on seemingly small or serendipitous factors. There is no question that the success of the Beatles, and the rise of Beatlemania, involved an informational cascade. We may doubt that in a counterfactual world there might have been Kinksmania or Holliesmania, but it would be reckless to rule out the possibility that some other band, obscure or unknown, might have taken the place of the Beatles.

Keywords: social influence, informational cascade, network effects, group polarization

> If we were to put ourselves in the place of their contemporaries and judge by the implicit standards of the public circa 1820, Keats would trail far behind Cornwall, and Hunt would lead the group [...] If we accepted the standards of professional critics of the time, Cornwall would outrank Hunt, and Keats would be in third place.
>
> H.J. Jackson (Jackson 2015: 163)

The Journal of Beatles Studies Autumn (2022) ISSN 2754-7019 (online)
https://doi.org/10.3828/jbs.2022.6
Published open access under a CC BY licence. https://creativecommons.org/licences/by/4.0/

A cheat

Yesterday, the brilliant 2019 film, asks a provocative question: what would happen in a world in which the Beatles had never existed, but in which one person, by some kind of magic, knows all their songs and delivers them afresh to that world? Much of the power of the film lies in its successful effort to encourage the audience to hear songs from the Beatles as if they were new — as if we were listening for the first time. What if we just heard, last night or this morning, 'I Saw Her Standing There', 'Let It Be', 'Yesterday', 'Carry That Weight', or 'Here Comes the Sun'? *Yesterday* invites viewers to ask that question and in a sense to experience the answer — to discover the Beatles all over again. More subtly and equally interestingly, the film contains a clear empirical hypothesis, which it makes plausible or perhaps irresistible: the Beatles were surpassingly great, and their sheer greatness was, and is, a guarantee of spectacular popularity, wherever and however their music emerged.

But in an important respect, the film is a cheat. The audience *already knows the songs.* We cannot unhear them. As we watch the movie unfold, we begin in a state of incredulity; we simply cannot believe that people are acting as if they have not heard, or have not even heard of, the Beatles. To be sure, we can try to experience the thrill of hearing their music as if it were fresh; the movie encourages us to do that. But unlike the audiences in the film, the songs are hardly new to us. We already love them. We do not need to be introduced to them. Hence the film does not establish its central claim: because of their amazing music, the success of the Beatles, and the rise of Beatlemania, were essentially inevitable.

An experiment on cultural success and failure

A number of years ago, social scientists Matthew Salganik, Duncan Watts and Peter Dodds investigated the sources of cultural success and failure (Salganik, Dodds and Watts 2006). Their starting point was that those who sell books, movies, television shows and songs often have a great deal of trouble predicting what will succeed. Even experts make serious mistakes. (As we shall see, these points hold for the Beatles, who had a hard time getting a record deal at all.) Some products are far more successful than anticipated, whereas some are far less so. This seems to suggest, very simply, that those that succeed must be far better than those that do not. But if they are so much better, why are predictions so difficult?

To explore the sources of cultural success and failure, Salganik and his co-authors created an artificial music market on a pre-existing website. The site offered people an opportunity to hear forty-eight real but unknown songs by real but unknown bands. One song, for example, by a band called Calefaction, was 'Trapped in an Orange Peel'. Another, by Hydraulic Sandwich, was 'Separation Anxiety'. The experimenters randomly sorted half of about 14,000 site visitors into an 'independent judgment' group, in which they were invited to listen to brief excerpts, to rate songs and to decide whether to download them. From those 7,000 visitors, Salganik and his co-authors could obtain a clear sense of what people liked best. The other 7,000 visitors were sorted into a 'social influence' group, which was exactly the same except in just one respect: the social influence group could see how many times each song had been downloaded by other participants.

Those in the social influence group were also randomly assigned to one of eight subgroups, in which they could see only the number of downloads in their own subgroup. In those different subgroups, it was inevitable that different songs would attract different initial numbers of downloads as a result of serendipitous or random factors. For example, 'Trapped in an Orange Peel' might attract strong support from the first listeners in one subgroup, whereas it might attract no such support in another. 'Separation Anxiety' might be unpopular in its first hours in one subgroup but attract a great deal of favourable attention in another. (For vividness, we might think of the experiment as testing the potential success or failure of Rory Storm and the Hurricanes, Freddie and the Dreamers, the Honeycombs and the Swinging Blue Jeans — bands from the 1960s that are not exactly famous today — and as comparing their potential success, in real time, to that of the Beatles, the Rolling Stones and the Dave Clark Five.)

The research questions were simple: would the initial numbers affect where songs would end up in terms of total number of downloads? Would the initial numbers affect the ultimate rankings of the forty-eight songs? Would the eight subgroups differ in those rankings? It might be hypothesized that after a period, quality would always prevail — that in this relatively simple setting, where various extraneous factors (such as reviews) were highly unlikely to be at work, the popularity of the songs, as measured by their download rankings, would be roughly the same in the independent group and in all eight of the social influence groups. (Recall that for purposes of the experiment, quality is being measured solely by reference to what happened within the control group.)

That is not what happened. 'Trapped in an Orange Peel' could be a major hit or a miserable flop, depending on whether a lot of other people initially downloaded it and were seen to have done so. To a significant degree, everything turned on initial popularity. Almost any song could end up popular or not, depending on whether or not the first visitors liked it. Importantly, there is one qualification relevant to the Beatles and to which I will return: the songs that did the very best in the independent judgment group rarely did very badly, and the songs that did the very worst in the independent judgment group rarely did spectacularly well. But otherwise, almost anything could happen. Salganik et al. urge that success and failure are exceedingly hard to predict and at least for one reason: it is difficult to know, in advance, whether a cultural product will benefit from the equivalent of early downloads.

For perspective, consider a tempting view: For one or another reason, some cultural products are genuinely destined for success and others are unquestionably doomed to failure. But before accepting that view, it is fair to ask: What, exactly, do these sentences mean? Let us simply suggest that we are really speaking of probabilities. Roughly: if history could be run 10,000 times, and if there were significant variations each time, success would happen, for some cultural products, almost all of the time, and failure would occur, for some cultural products, essentially all of the time. But that apparent clarification raises many questions of its own. If history is being rerun, what are we changing, and what are we holding constant? Let us venture, then, a more specific and also cautious claim: if a song, a novel or a poem is truly sensational, it will almost certainly be recognized as such, and if a song, a novel or poem is truly terrible, it will disappear. The Beatles, Bob Dylan, Taylor Swift, Charles Dickens, Thomas Hardy and John Keats were essentially bound for success simply because of their quality. Recall that the songs that did the very best in the independent judgement group rarely did very badly. And if a song, a novel or a poem is horrible, it will not do well. (Of course, we would need to specify the criteria for a conclusion that something is sensational or horrible; let us simply make a stipulation here.) But within a wide range, songs can do very well or very poorly, and within that range, predictions are hazardous. For music (and much else), everything might seem to depend on social influences (Bikhchandani, Hirshleifer and Welch 1992; Jackson 2015).

In light of the Salganik et al. findings, even this view, while plausible, might be too cautious about the role of social influences, and too confident about the role of quality. To be sure, terrible songs and terrible works of literature are unlikely to succeed (with occasional horrifying exceptions). But perhaps the best ones are hardly destined for success. After all, the Salganik et al. experiment itself was tightly controlled. It tested only forty-eight songs. In real markets there are countless more. And in those real-world markets, media attention, critical acclaim, marketing, product placement and sheer luck play a significant role. With these points in mind, suppose that in an experimental setting, 'Trapped in an Orange Peel' almost always does well, and 'Separation Anxiety' almost never does. It does not follow that if 'Trapped in an Orange Peel' is released to the public, the song will be a large success, or that 'Separation Anxiety' will fail. At least above a certain threshold of quality, everything might turn out to depend on the range of social influences that follow the release.

As a possible demonstration of the point, consider the tale told in 2012, when the Oscar for best documentary was awarded to *Searching for Sugar Man*. The film focused on an unsuccessful

Detroit singer-songwriter named Sixto Rodriguez, also known as Sugar Man, who released two albums in the early 1970s. Almost no one bought his albums, and his label dropped him. Not surprisingly, Rodriguez stopped making records and sought work as a demolition man. His two albums were forgotten. A family man with three daughters, Rodriguez was hardly miserable. But working in demolition, he struggled.

The film suggests that having abandoned his musical career, Rodriguez had no idea that he had become a spectacular success in South Africa — a giant, a legend, comparable to the Beatles and the Rolling Stones. People said his name slowly and with awe, even reverence: 'Rodriguez'. Describing him as 'the soundtrack to our lives', South Africans bought hundreds of thousands of copies of his albums, starting in the 1970s. His South African fans speculated about his mysterious departure from the musical scene. Why did he suddenly stop making records? According to one rumour, he burned himself to death onstage. *Searching for Sugar Man* is about the contrast between the failed career of Detroit's obscure demolition man and the renown of South Africa's mysterious rock icon.

The film is easily taken as a real-world fairy tale and barely believable. It does not attempt to give an explanation for the contrast between Rodriguez's general failure and his extraordinary success in South Africa. We might be tempted to think that (for example) his music resonated with South African culture. Perhaps so. But an alternative explanation is that *Searching for Sugar Man* depicts a real-life version of the Salganik et al. experiment. Perhaps Rodriguez found himself in counterfactual worlds, and because of an absence of early downloads in most, he was forgotten in nearly all of them. But in one, early downloads were numerous, and he became an icon.

Informational cascades

There is, of course, a great deal of work, in many fields, on the topic of cultural success and failure, and on the respective roles of success, talent, hard work, fit with the times, marketing and luck (for a small sampling, see Bikhchandani et al. 1992; Banks 2017; Rosen 1981; Menger 2014; Williams, Lacasa and Latora 2019). I do not attempt here to offer a survey or to integrate the diverse perspectives illuminatingly reflected in the relevant research. My more modest goal is to isolate what seem to me to be the most important strands that bear on the roles of social influences and serendipity (understanding that term to be an umbrella concept), and to bring them to bear on the success of the Beatles in particular.

What Salganik et al. uncovered was a set of *informational cascades*, a phenomenon that helps illuminate what happened during Beatlemania (and in the decades since) (Berman 2008). The starting point is that people rationally attend to the informational signals given by the statements and action of others; we amplify the volume of the very signals by which we have been influenced. Social movements of various kinds, including fads, fashions and rebellions (bellbottoms, the rise of the Monkees, the popularity of Jane Austen and the *Mona Lisa*, the Arab Spring, #MeToo, the attack on Critical Race Theory) can be understood as a product of cascade effects.

To see how informational cascades work, imagine that seven people are in a reading group, deciding which book to try next. Assume that group members are announcing their views in sequence. Each person attends, reasonably enough, to the judgements of others. John is the first to speak. He suggests that a new book about the Beatles is the one to try. Paul, the second to speak, now knows John's judgement; he should certainly go along with John's recommendation if he is also enthusiastic about that book. But suppose that he does not really know; he is indifferent. If Paul trusts John, he might simply agree that the group should choose that new book.

Now turn to a third person, George. Suppose after both John and Paul have said that they want to try the book about the Beatles, George's own view, based on his own limited information, is that the book is not likely to be very good. Even if George has that view, he might well ignore what he knows and just follow John and Paul. The reason is not that George is humble or cowardly. It is likely, after all, that both John and Paul have reasons for their enthusiasm.

Unless George thinks that his own information is genuinely better than theirs, he ought to follow their lead. If he does, George is in a cascade. True, George will resist if he has sufficient grounds to think that John and Paul are being foolish. But if he lacks those grounds, he is likely to go along with them.

Now suppose that Ringo, Brian, Yoko and Linda are expected to express their views. If John, Paul and George have all said that the new book on the Beatles is the one to read, each of them might well reach the same conclusion (in sequence) even if they have some independent reason to think another choice would be better. In this example, the most important point is that the initial judgement by only one person (John) initiated a process by which some people are led to participate in a cascade, leading the entire group to opt for a particular book. If John had suggested otherwise, or if Ringo had spoken first, the group might have made a different choice.

This is, of course, a highly artificial and stylized example. But the basic process should be familiar, and it helps explain what happened in the Salganik et al. experiment. People learn from others, and if some people seem to like something or to want to do something, others might like or do the same. This is so unless they have some reason to distrust them and if they lack a good reason to think that they are wrong.

It is important to emphasize that economic models of informational cascades generally assume rational behaviour. If one does not know whether a book, a movie, a group or a song is good, it might well be reasonable to rely on the views of others, at least if you trust them (or do not distrust them). As the number of people who share the same view increases, relying on them becomes more reasonable still. The idea of the 'wisdom of crowds' lies in this insight (Sunstein 2006). Nonetheless, there are problems. People tend to neglect the possibility that most of the people in the crowd might be in a cascade too. and are not making independent judgements of their own (Eyster and Rabin 2010). Ringo might think that John, Paul and George have all decided that a particular book is the one to read, when in fact John is the only person who has made that judgement. When observers see a dozen, a hundred, ten thousand or two million people doing something, they might well underestimate the extent to which people are simply following their predecessors.

It is also important to see that while informational cascades might produce large-scale changes in belief and behaviour, they might not be entirely rational (Kuran and Sunstein 1999), and also that they might not be robust. If John was wrong to select the new book about the Beatles, and if the book was truly terrible, he will learn that he was wrong, and so will the rest of the group's members. An informational cascade might lead people to download songs, to start to read a book, or to go to a movie theatre, but can it actually lead people to *like* songs, books, or movies? The best answer is 'no', but it is too simple. It is true that if people can tell that a song is terrible or dull, they will not enjoy it, even if they think that others have, and eventually, the song's popularity will wane. In this sense, informational cascades can be fragile. But for songs or other cultural products that rise above a certain quality threshold, we cannot rule out the possibility that the reality or perception of widespread enthusiasm will lead to enduring success.

Consider in this regard a different experiment, also from Salganik and his collaborators (Salganik and Watts 2008). This experiment drew on the experiment previously described, but with one exception: the experimenters inverted the actual download figures, so that participants would think that the least popular songs were the most popular, and the most popular songs the least. If quality is the real driver, one might expect that the worst songs (as measured by the independent judgement group) would eventually plummet to the bottom, and that the best ones (also as so measured) would eventually rise to the top. Not at all. With the inversion, Salganik and Watts transformed the worst songs into significant successes and could also make almost all of the top songs into colossal failures. Here, as in their principal experiment, the lesson is that people pay a great deal of attention to what other people appear to like, and that information about popularity can make all the difference. The wrinkle is that the very best songs (again, as measured by actual popularity in the independent judgement tradition) always ended up doing quite well; social influences could not keep them down (though they could prevent them from being ranked at the very top).

Reputational cascades

With cultural products, people may pay attention to the views of others because they want to know what is good. But sometimes what they most want is for other people to like them, or at least not to dislike them. They follow the views and actions of others for that reason. If most people are enthusiastic about a new song or movie, they might show enthusiasm as well, or at least listen or look. We might do what others do because they are giving us a signal about what is good or right or true, but we might also conform because we care what they think about us (Sunstein 2002).

In a reputational cascade, people think that they know what is right, or what is likely to be right, but they nonetheless go along with the crowd in order to maintain the good opinion of others (Kuran 1998). Suppose that Mick suggests that the Dave Clark Five is spectacular and that Keith concurs with Mick, not because he actually thinks that Mick is right, but because he does not wish to seem to Mick to be some kind of fool or idiot. If Mick and Keith say that the Dave Clark Five is terrific, Brian might not contradict them publicly and might even appear to share their judgement. This is not because he believes that judgement to be correct, but because he does not want to face their hostility or lose their good opinion.

It should be easy to see how this process might generate a cascade on behalf of the Dave Clark Five. Once Mick, Keith and Brian offer a united front on the issue, their friend Charlie might be reluctant to contradict them even if he thinks that they are wrong. The apparently shared view of Mick, Keith and Brian carries information; that view might be right. But even if Charlie has reason to believe that they are wrong, he might not want to take them on publicly. His own silence will help build the reputational pressure on those who follow. In the Salganik et al. (2006) experiments, visitors to the site were not likely to be concerned about how their downloads affected their reputations. They were not necessarily friends or even acquaintances with one another. But when groups of people embrace a product, it is often because of the social pressure that comes from the apparent views of others.

Network effects

Some things can be enjoyed by oneself. You might like a walk in the sun, a cup of coffee or a quick swim, even or perhaps especially if you are alone. Other pleasures are guilty. One might love a silly television show and the music of Tommy Roe, and one might not want to watch the show or listen to Tommy Roe with anyone else. But sometimes the value of a good depends on how many other people are using or enjoying it (De Giorgi, Frederiksen and Pistaferri 2020; Sunstein and Ullmann-Margalit 2001). It is not worthwhile to have a cell phone if you are the only person in the world who has a cell phone. People use Facebook because many people use Facebook. If Facebook had not been able to build a network, it would have failed. Network effects exist when value increases with the number of users.

Some cultural products benefit greatly from network effects: they are taken as something of which people think they should be aware. Quite apart from the intrinsic merits of a song or a television show, it might be good to know about it so that one can talk to others about it. It might not be a lot of fun to stare blankly when someone makes a knowing reference to 'Yesterday', 'Hey Jude' or 'Let It Be', or even to 'For No One'. If people see that other people like the Beatles and focus on them, they might join them for one reason above all: they do not want to be left out. They want to be part of the relevant group.

When books and movies benefit from exploding popularity, it is often because of network effects. John Lennon faced a horrific backlash when he remarked that the Beatles had become 'more popular than Jesus', but he was capturing the existence of network effects, from which the Beatles greatly benefited. Taylor Swift is terrific, but she is a massive success in part because people want to be part of the ever-growing group of people who know about, and like or love, Taylor Swift.

Group polarization

Group polarization is among the most robust patterns found in deliberating bodies, and it has been found in many diverse tasks (Sunstein 2019; Brown 1983). The result is that groups often make more extreme decisions than would the typical or average individual in the group (where 'extreme' is defined solely internally, by reference to the group's initial dispositions). For cultural products, the implication of group polarization is strong: like-minded people, engaged in discussions with one another, will end up pushing one another to extremes, potentially including 'manias' of various sorts. (Beatlemania is just one illustration, and it is not the most extreme.)

Consider some examples of the basic phenomenon, which has been found in over a dozen nations (Sunstein 2019; Zuber, Crott and Werner 1992; Abrams et al. 1990). The relevant work has been undertaken for more than fifty years, and the central findings have been found to be quite robust:

(a) After discussion, Americans who are concerned about climate change, and favour an international treaty to control it, become more firmly committed to those beliefs (Sunstein 2019).

(b) After discussion, Americans who are not especially concerned about climate change, and do not favour an international treaty to control it, become even less enthusiastic about such a treaty (ibid.).

(c) After discussion, citizens of France become more critical of the United States and its intentions with respect to economic aid (Brown 1983: 224).

(d) A group of moderately pro-feminist women will become more strongly pro-feminist after discussion with one another (Myers 1975: 710–712).

(e) After discussion, whites predisposed to show racial prejudice offer more negative responses to the question whether white racism is responsible for conditions faced by African-Americans in American cities (Myers and Bishop 1970).

(f) After discussion, whites predisposed not to show racial prejudice offer more positive responses to the same question (ibid.).

As statistical regularities, it follows, for example, that those moderately enthusiastic about a poem, a movie, a song or a novel will, after discussion, grow in their enthusiasm. (Consider Beatlemania in this light, and note that concerts are often case studies in group polarization.) Of course it is also true that some people may remain outliers, either because they really do not like the direction in which the group is going (and are willing to say so), or because they are rebels by nature.

There are three main explanations for why group polarization occurs (Sunstein 2019; Brown 1983: 210–225), and all of them bear on the evaluation of poems, movies, songs and novels. The first points to the relationship among corroboration, confidence and extremism (Baron et al. 1996; Heath and Gonzales 1995). Those who lack confidence, and who are unsure what they should think, tend to moderate their views. It is for this reason that cautious people, not knowing what to do, are likely to choose the midpoint between relevant extremes. But if other people seem to share one's view, one is likely to become more confident that that view is right – and hence to move in a more extreme direction. Enthusiasm for musicians, artists and writers often intensifies in this way. (The Beatles are a case in point, and so are the Doors, to point to just one other; their fans seemed to participate in a process of group polarization.)

The second explanation emphasizes the role of information exchange (Bishop and Myers 1974). It is based on a simple claim: any individual's position on an issue is partly a function of what information is presented, and of which arguments presented within the group seem convincing. The choice therefore moves in the direction of the most persuasive position defended by the group, taken as a whole. Because a group whose members are already inclined in a certain direction will have a disproportionate number of arguments supporting that same direction, the result of discussion will be to move people further in the direction of their initial inclinations.

The final explanation begins with the claim that people want to be perceived favourably by other group members, and also to perceive themselves favourably (Sunstein 2002). Once they hear what others believe, they adjust their positions in the direction of the dominant position. They may want to signal, for example, that they are not cowardly or cautious. Thus individuals move their judgements in order to preserve their image to others and their image to themselves. Is Beatlemania an illustration? No doubt about it.

'Here lies one whose name was writ in water'

Can social dynamics help to explain the success of cultural figures? Of poets, novelists and musicians? Of John Milton, John Updike, Joni Mitchell, Aimee Mann and Steve Earle? This is an exceedingly difficult question to answer. To do so, we would need to specify the hypothesis we mean to test, and then we would need to test it. The category of social influences is large and diverse; it includes not only initial popularity, but also prominent reviewers, well-known or wealthy sponsors, perceived identity (do young people like x or y? do rebellious people like x or y?) and conventions of form, all of which will vary over time and place. In one nation, Mitchell, Mann or Earle might resonate immediately, because they build on, or perhaps deliver an intriguing shock to, something that is liked and familiar. In another nation, one or all might be barely intelligible.

Salganik and his collaborators were able to test a clear hypothesis: Would the popularity of songs be affected by social influences, so that download rankings would vary across subgroups? To undertake a comparable test, we might identify a set of novelists (say, Thomas Hardy, Charles Dickens, Jane Austen, James Joyce, George Orwell, A.S. Byatt, Joyce Carol Oates and Stephen King), treat them like songs, and see whether groups, in conditions like those in Salganik et al. (2006), would produce similar rankings. It would certainly be possible to do something like that with unknown novelists. Because Hardy, Dickens, Austen and the rest are widely known, it would be much harder to do that with them, or to see how they might be compared to lesser known novelists, either in their times or ours. History is not a randomized controlled experiment; it is run only once. For that reason, it is not easy to know how we might test the role of informational cascades with respect to poems, novels, music and the like, or even to specify the hypothesis we are testing (a point to which I will return).

Nonetheless, H.J. Jackson's important study of literary reputation offers important clues, and it strongly suggests that accident, contingency and luck play a massive role (Jackson 2015: 1–24). Jackson explores, among other things, the twists and turns that led to the canonization of William Wordsworth, John Keats, Jane Austen and William Blake, and the contrastingly lower reputations of George Crabbe, Robert Southey, Barry Cornwall, Leigh Hunt and Mary Brunton. In a sense, Jackson can be read as making the provocative argument that over a much longer time scale, Wordsworth, Keats, Austen and Blake were like successful songs in the Salganik et al. study, and that Crabbe, Southey, Cornwall, Hunt and Brunton were akin to the unsuccessful ones (ibid.: 167–217). Are the Beatles in some respects like Keats? Are the Kinks in some respects like Cornwall? We will get to that.

In terms of perceived quality, Jackson finds that Keats, Cornwall and Hunt were grouped together during their lifetimes. The same is true of Wordsworth, Crabbe and Southey, and also of Austen and Brunton (ibid.: 63–107). If one asked their contemporaries which names, of these eight, would be most famous in the twenty-first century, there would be no consensus in favour of Keats, Wordsworth and Austen. In particular, Jackson notes that Keats might well count as the most beloved poet of all time – but at the time of his death, he believed that he had utterly failed in his somewhat desperate quest for literary fame. Indeed, he left instructions that his gravestone have no name, but only these pathetic words: '[h]ere lies one whose name was writ in water' (ibid.: 115). In Keats's time, Cornwall was far more successful;

he was regarded as the great poet while Keats was met with 'indifference or hostility'.

Tracing Keats's improbable rise to prominence decades after his death, Jackson writes, 'It seems that his reputation was dependent less on the efforts of particular individuals than on groups, overlapping networks of like-minded acquaintances starting up on a small scale, the collective chatter that later becomes the buzz of fame' (ibid.: 117). (Informational cascades, reputational cascades, network effects, and group polarization are all relevant here.) In terms of pure poetic quality, Jackson urges, Cornwall's virtues and vices greatly overlap with those of Keats. Jackson's remarkable conclusion, which she makes quite plausible, is that '[a]s far as reputation is concerned, the differences between them are largely personal and accidental' (ibid.). At the very least, it is necessary to come to terms with the 'conundrum of Barry Cornwall's success with the same audience that spurned Keats' (ibid.: 155). Indeed, their contemporaries put Cornwall far above Keats; Hunt ranked above them both. And if we are interested in professional opinions, we will find that Wordsworth, Samuel Taylor Coleridge and Lord Byron all ranked Cornwall highest of the three. As Jackson (2015: 40–41) puts it:

> An overview of the history of the reception of Wordsworth's work offers little support for his theory of the autonomous isolated genius who generates works of overwhelming intrinsic merit and wins readers over one at a time until the enlightened audience achieves critical mass. On the contrary, it reveals a process of regular reinterpretation involving, at every turn, the vital initiative of other agents.

It might be tempting, of course, to say that history should be seen as a market, and that ultimate success went to the best. On this view, the system worked. But perhaps not. How would we know, exactly? In terms of changing reputations over time, Jackson places a particular emphasis on echo chamber effects, which can consolidate a writer's image. In their time, Mary Brunton and Jane Austen were about equally well regarded, but the former of course faded into obscurity. Jackson urges, and makes it plausible to think, that what 'happened to Brunton — the gradual fading and extinction of her name — could easily have happened to Austen' (2015: 95). The long-obscure Blake himself was a beneficiary of a highly improbable and complex recovery project, barely rescuing him from literary oblivion. (Did something like that happen, very quickly, to the Beatles? We will get to that.) In his time, his works 'were almost unknown to his contemporaries' (ibid.: 168).

Jackson's conclusion is that, notwithstanding 'the common assumption that over time, the best writers come out on top, the reception histories [...] show that long-term survival has depended more on external circumstances and accidental advantages than on inherent literary worth' (2015: 218). Perhaps the most famous literary figures are, in fact, greater than those who are unknown; we would be strongly inclined to think so. How could we not? But perhaps we are wrong. A modest suggestion is that with a little push or shove, or download equivalents at the right time, the literary canon could feature Crabbe, Hunt and Brunton.

'The boys won't go'

Let us now return to the hypothesis of *Yesterday*: because of the intrinsic quality of their songs, Beatlemania was inevitable. If people now heard 'I Saw Her Standing There', 'Let It Be' or 'Hey Jude' for the first time, they would immediately recognize that they were hearing something extraordinary. It would not matter whether people heard such songs in 1954, 1964, 1974, 1984, 1994, 2004 or 2044. It would not matter if people heard those songs as individuals, and in a way that could not possibly be affected by social influences, or if they heard those songs in groups consisting mostly of people largely predisposed, for one or another reason, to like them.

On an alternative account, *Yesterday*'s hypothesis is far too simple; social influences in general and cascade effects in particular were crucial to the rise of Beatlemania. By itself, this alternative claim is too vague to be a testable hypothesis; it could take various forms. On the weakest (and perhaps trivial) version, the Beatles' success was indeed inevitable in light of their genius, but it occurred in the precise way that it did, and with the speed it did, because, when and where they received the equivalent of a large number of early downloads. On that view, there are plausible counterfactual worlds in which the Beatles ultimately succeeded, just as in our world, but in which that success unfolded at different speeds and in intriguingly different ways. This claim is indeed relatively trivial, and we should be immediately able to see why. Indeed, it is consistent with what I have called the hypothesis of *Yesterday*.

A stronger version is much bolder and not at all trivial. On that view, there is a counterfactual world in which the Beatles did not get the equivalent of a large number of initial downloads, and they ultimately gave up. In that counterfactual world, the Beatles might have been the equivalent of 'Trapped in an Orange Peel', writ large. That world would be something like the world of *Yesterday*. Indeed, it might actually *be* the world of *Yesterday* (which never explains why, exactly, the Beatles never made it there). If so, the mystery of the movie would be simple to state if not to solve: why would the Beatles' songs do spectacularly well now, when the group failed in the 1960s?

The plausibility of the strong version of the social influence account is difficult to test, because (one more time) history is only run once. We do not have anything like a randomized controlled trial, or a number of counterfactual worlds. The best and perhaps the only way to evaluate the hypothesis is through close investigation of the actual history — the only one we have — in search of clues. Consider the elaborate discussion by Mark Lewisohn, whose book captures a series of serendipitous events that made the group's success possible, and which gestures toward counterfactual worlds in which Beatlemania would have never come into existence (Lewisohn 2013: 489—515). In a sense, we could read Lewisohn's account as a temporally compressed cousin to Jackson's study of literary reputation (Jackson 2015). As Lewisohn describes in detail, the young group initially became quite popular in local clubs in Liverpool but struggled mightily to attract wider attention. Social influences were not (sufficiently) in their favour. Lacking a manager, and with only modest prospects, they came close to splitting up in 1961, fearing they were unlikely to succeed (Lewisohn 2013: 397–489). Eventually they asked two young secretaries, who were helping to run their Liverpool fan club, to manage the group. But the secretaries found it exceedingly hard to get them bookings.

The group's initial break came when Brian Epstein, the 27-year-old manager of a Liverpool record store, happened to hear them at a lunchtime session at a club. Epstein loved them and decided they would be 'bigger than Elvis'. Improbably, he offered to manage them. He did so even though he lacked relevant experience and even though the Beatles had become exceedingly unpopular with promoters and were, in Lewisohn's words, 'damaged goods', known for 'being unreliable, unpunctual, arrogant' (Lewisohn 2013: 505). At first Epstein's efforts proved futile. EMI, a prominent British recording company, refused to give the Beatles a contract. Epstein obtained an opportunity for them to test for Decca, EMI's rival, but the group's performance was terrible, and it too turned them down. 'The boys won't go', the company's representatives informed Epstein. 'We know these things. You have a good record business in Liverpool. Stick to that' (ibid.: 558).

The Beatles were stunned by Decca's rejection. John Lennon said they thought 'that was the end'. In Paul McCartney's words, 'It was all a bit bloody hell, what are we gonna do?' (Lewisohn 2013: 591). Epstein ended up seeing every potential record company, and *every one of them refused to sign the Beatles*. In apparent desperation, Epstein went back to EMI, where he played a Beatles tape for producer George Martin, who was unimpressed. Martin saw 'a rather raw group' with 'a pretty lousy tape' and 'not very good songs' (ibid.: 571). That might have concluded matters except for the intervention of two people, Kim Bennett and Sid Colman, who worked for one of EMI's music publishing companies. Epstein had played some Beatles music for Bennett and Colman, who liked what they heard. In a highly unusual move, Colman offered to pay EMI for the cost of recording a Beatles record. But the resulting session, overseen by an unenthusiastic Martin, went poorly, and he decided not to issue any of the songs. He later confessed, 'I didn't think the Beatles had any songs of any worth. They gave me no evidence whatsoever that they could write hit material' (ibid.: 647).

When the group came back into the studio, he did not like them much better, but he reluctantly concluded that 'Love Me Do' should be released as a single. He had little confidence in it, and when he mentioned the group's bizarre name to his EMI colleagues, they broke out into laughter. EMI refused to support the song. In Martin's words, 'Nobody believed in it at all' (Lewisohn 2013: 717). 'Love Me Do' might have dropped like a stone, along with the Beatles' prospects, except for Epstein's relentlessness (and the use of his own money for promotion). The group's enthusiastic fan base in Liverpool ended up buying the record and started an informational cascade. Despite mixed reviews, Epstein's pushing helped make the song into an unexpected hit. At this point, Martin, the original sceptic, made an astounding decision. He decided to ask the Beatles to record a real album, consisting mostly of Lennon–McCartney songs. Martin turned out, of course, to be a brilliant producer, perfectly matched to the fledgling group.

There are many paths to success, and perhaps the Beatles would have found one even without Epstein, Bennett, Colman and Martin. Lennon himself thought so, insisting that the Beatles were the best group in the world (using expletives between *best* and *world*). 'Believing that is what made us what we were', he said. 'It was just a matter of time before everybody caught on' (Lewisohn 2013: 803). Perhaps so; evidently John accepted the hypothesis of *Yesterday*. But Lewisohn's own account suggests the possibility of counterfactual worlds, not testing any hypothesis but raising the intriguing possibility that the Beatles' success was anything but foreordained. And indeed the word 'foreordained' raises many puzzles. For example: What if Paul had met John at some other time? What if John had been in an especially sour mood on the fateful day?

To be sure, it is important to emphasize that in Lewisohn's account, many of the serendipitous factors had nothing to do with social influences and informational cascades. Epstein's involvement and enthusiasm might have been essential (we do not know), but it might be a stretch to see it as the functional equivalent of early downloads (how much of a stretch, though?), and the same is true for the involvement of Bennett and Colman. Still, and crucially, a failure to obtain (sufficient) early popularity in 1961 almost doomed the Beatles. How close did it come? We do not know. In addition, something very much like a large number of early downloads for 'Love Me Do' in 1963 made all the difference. Was it essential to the Beatles' success? We do not know that either.

'Lost Einsteins'

Would it be possible, in this light, to imagine a counterfactual world in which the Beatles did not make it? A counterfactual world without the Beatles, and instead with other bandmanias — say, Kinksmania or Holliesmania? With a new *Journal of Hollies Studies*? These questions seem preposterous. The Beatles' enduring success — their rediscovery by successive generations, their spectacular success in various years long after they broke up — can be taken to support the idea that they were unique, and that their uniqueness made their success essentially inevitable. Then there is the question of sheer quality, which is not my topic here, but which is surely relevant. To be sure, Ray Davies is inventive and original (consider 'Lola'), and Graham Nash is better than good (consider 'Our House'), but neither of them could be put in the same category as Lennon or McCartney. But it is important to be careful on this topic, and on several different counts. First, Lennon and McCartney were not, in 1961 or even 1963, the Lennon and McCartney we now know. Their early success was almost certainly a necessary condition for the flowering of what we rightly see as their genius. Second, we do not know what Davies, Nash or many others might have done, or might have been, if they had had the extraordinary success of the Beatles in the early 1960s.

To be sure, it seems implausible to suggest that the Beatles needed early downloads to succeed, or that Davies or Nash, or someone of whom we have never heard, could have been Lennon or McCartney. Of course cascade effects played a large role, and so did network effects, and so did group polarization. But these claims are consistent with what I have described as a weak or trivial account of the role of social influences. In my view, and with fear and trembling, a plausible conclusion is that the Beatles should be seen as analytically equivalent to the very best songs in the Salganik et al. experiment, and in the end, they would have found a way, at least in a very large number of counterfactual worlds.

But that proposition cannot be proved. Is it an article of faith? Perhaps so (Jackson 2015). To vindicate the proposition, we would need to say much more about the content of those counterfactual worlds, and how, exactly, they differ from our own; a great deal remains to be done on this count. And with respect to bandmanias that never were, consider the fact that in the domain of innovation in general, empirical work points to 'Lost Einsteins' (Bell et al. 2019; Williams 2019) — to those 'who would have had highly impactful inventions had they been exposed to innovation in childhood' (Bell et al. 2019). In this work, the emphasis is on demographic characteristics, such as race, gender and socio-economic status, and on the contributions of role models and network effects to success. We cannot entirely rule out the possibility that there are lost Lennons, lost McCartneys and lost bands that might have turned out to be comparable to the Beatles. If they have been lost, it is not only because of demographic characteristics, but also because of social influences, which did not work in their favour.

Acknowledgements

I am grateful to Tyler Cowen and Duncan Watts for valuable comments and discussions, and to Eric Xu for superb research assistance. Some parts of this article draw on my previous work on social influences and informational cascades, including Cass R. Sunstein, *Conformity* (2019).

Bibliography

Abrams, Dominic, Margaret Wetherell, Sandra Cochrane, Michael A. Hogg and John C. Turner (1990) 'Knowing what to think by knowing who you are: self-categorization and the nature of norm formation, conformity and group polarization', *British Journal of Social Psychology* 29(2): 97–119, doi:10.1111/j.2044-8309.1990.tb00892.x.
Banks, Mark (2017) *Creative Justice* (London: Rowman & Littlefield).

Baron, Robert S., Sieg I. Hoppe, C.F. Kao, B.M. Brunsman, B. Linneweh and D. Rogers (1996) 'Social collaboration and opinion extremity', *Journal of Experimental Social Psychology* 32(6): 537–560, doi:10.1006/jesp.1996/0024.

Bell, Alex, Raj Chetty, Xavier Jaravel, Neviana Petkova and John van Reenen (2019) 'Who becomes an inventor in America? The importance of exposure to innovation', *Quarterly Journal of Economics* 134(2): 647–713, doi:10.1093/qje/qjy028.

Bendjelloul, Malik (dir.) (2012) *Searching for Sugar Man*.

Berman, Garry (2008) *'We're Going to See the Beatles!'* (Santa Monica: Santa Monica Press).

Bikhchandani, Sushil, David Hirshleifer and Ivo Welch (1992) 'A theory of fads, custom, and cultural change as informational cascades', *The Journal of Political Economy* 100(5): 992–1026, doi:0022-3808/92/0005-0001.

Bishop, George D. and David G. Myers (1974) 'Informational influences in group discussion', *Organizational Behavior and Human Performance* 12: 92–104.

Boyle, Danny (dir.) (2019) *Yesterday*.

Brown, Roger (1983) *Social Psychology: The Second Edition* (New York: Free Press).

De Giorgi, Giacomo, Anders Frederiksen and Luigi Pistaferri (2020) 'Consumption network effects', *Review of Economic Studies* 87: 130–163, doi:10.1093/restud/rdz026.

Eyster, Erik and Matthew Rabin (2010) 'Naïve herding in rich-information settings', *American Economic Journal: Microeconomics* 2: 221–243, doi:10.1257/mic.2.4.221.

Heath, Chip and Rich Gonzalez (1995) 'Interaction with others increases decision confidence but not decision quality: evidence against information collection views of interactive decision making', *Organizational Behavior and Human Decision Processes* 61(3): 305–326, doi:0749-5978/95.

Jackson, H.J. (2015) *Those Who Write for Immortality: Romantic Reputations and the Dream of Lasting Fame* (New Haven, CT: Yale University Press).

Kuran, Timur (1998) 'Ethnic norms and their transformation through reputational cascades', *The Journal of Legal Studies* 27(S2): 623–659, doi:0047-2530/98/2702-0017.

Kuran, Timur and Cass R. Sunstein (1999) 'Availability cascades and risk regulation', *Stanford Law Review* 51: 683–768.

Lewisohn, Mark (2013) *The Beatles: All These Years*, i: *Tune-In* (New York: Three Rivers Press).

Menger, Pierre-Michel (2014) *The Economics of Creativity: Art and Achievement under Uncertainty* (Cambridge, MA: Harvard University Press).

Myers, David G. (1975) 'Discussion-induced attitude polarization', *Human Relations* 28: 699–714, doi:10.1177/001872677502800802.

Myers, David G. and George D. Bishop (1970) 'Discussion effects on racial attitudes', *Science* 169: 778–779, doi:10.1126/science.169.3947.778.

Rosen, Sherwin (1981) 'The economics of superstars', *American Economic Review* 71(5): 845–58.

Salganik, Matthew J., Peter Sheridan Dodds and Duncan J. Watts (2006) 'Experimental study of inequality and unpredictability in an artificial cultural market', *Science* 311: 854–856, doi: 10.1126/science.1121066.

Salganik, Matthew J. and Duncan J. Watts (2008) 'Leading the herd astray: an experimental study of self-fulfilling prophecies in an artificial cultural market', *Social Psychology Quarterly* 71(4): 338–355.

Sunstein, Cass R. (2002) 'The law of group polarization', *Journal of Political Philosophy* 10(2): 175–195.

Sunstein, Cass R. (2006) *Infotopia: How Many Minds Produce Knowledge* (Oxford: Oxford University Press).

Sunstein, Cass R. (2019) *Conformity: The Power of Social Influences* (New York: New York University Press).

Sunstein, Cass R. and Edna Ullmann-Margalit (2001) 'Solidarity goods', *Journal of Political Philosophy* 9(2): 129–149, doi:10.1111/1467-9760.00121.

Williams, Heidi (2019) 'What inventions are we missing', *NBER Reporter* 1, https://www.nber.org/reporter/2019number1/what-inventions-are-we-missing (accessed 26 August 2022).

Williams, Oliver E., Lucas Lacasa and Vito Latora (2019) 'Quantifying and predicting success in show business', *Nature Communications* 10(1): 2256.

Zuber, J.A., H.W. Crott and Joachim Werner (1992) 'Choice shift and group polarization: an analysis of the status of arguments and social decision schemes', *Journal of Personality and Social Psychology* 62(1): 50–61, doi:10.1037/0022-3514.62.1.50.

Across the Universe

A lucky, good historian: notes on Lizzie Bravo's *Do Rio a Abbey Road* (*From Rio to Abbey Road*)

Paul Long

> *In the fog and in the rain / Through the pleasures
> and the pain / On the step outside you stand /
> With your flowers in your hand, my Apple Scruffs.*

George Harrison

In the 1969 *New Yorker* short story 'The Girl Who Sang with the Beatles', Robert Hemenway (writing under the pen name Stephen Patch) describes the role of the group's music in maintaining the relationship of Larry and Cynthia, the titular singer. Dramatizing a familiar trope in explanations of the band's success in the U.S.A., the Beatles come into the lives of the couple as a balm to their grieving over the death of John F. Kennedy. In fact, as a result of her engaged listening, Cynthia develops a rich imaginative life involving the band in which she is recruited to their ranks — another *fifth* Beatle — to sing and play guitar as part of their live performances. She acts out the scenario of this participation every night, aided by singing and playing along to records, telling Larry that when she's 'Beatling': 'I'm really there. It's more real than here. I know it's a fantasy though' (1969: 32).

Hemenway's portrait of Cynthia's agency as a cultural aficionado is a real curiosity in that moment of the group's life. She makes for an atypical portrait of a female fan when compared with the contemporary pathologizing of teenage 'Beatlemania'. Likewise, she contrasts with the salacious detailing of the role and duties

The Journal of Beatles Studies Autumn (2022)   ISSN 2754-7019 (online)
https://doi.org/10.3828/jbs.2022.7
Published open access under a CC BY licence. https://creativecommons.org/licences/by/4.0/

of the 'groupie', described as 'a chick who hangs out with bands' in the following month's *Rolling Stone* (Hopkins, Burks and Nelson 1969). Cynthia is woman in her thirties who is experienced in life, having worked as a singer and dancer while Larry is her second husband. Suggestive is how her imagined relationship with the band involves their meeting and developing a mutual liking for each other, leading *them* to recognize *her* talent and its value for their music. This fantasy is nonetheless entirely routinized, domesticated and made an everyday and thus sustaining experience for both Cynthia and Larry.

Lizzie Bravo, who died in 2021, was a fan lauded in obituaries as the girl who really *did* sing with the Beatles, appearing on the first version of 'Across the Universe' which was recorded in 1968 and released on the charity compilation *No One's Gonna Change Our World* the following year. That event, her agency and life as a Beatles fan is manifest in her memoir *Do Rio a Abbey Road* (*From Rio to Abbey Road*), self-published in 2015 in an initial print run of 1000 copies. Bravo's website describes the book's lovingly designed and curated presentation, which comprises 300 pages and over 200 unpublished photos of the Beatles with an introduction by Mark Lewisohn, 'the greatest Beatles authority on the planet!' She emphasized its personalized insights:

> These adventures are told in my teenage diaries, in the day-to-day life of following the Beatles wherever they were. Dressing room, accessories, objects, dialogues … all noted in detail. Unusual stories that would be unthinkable in today's world, which show how accessible and simple the Beatles were. (Bravo n.d., my translation)

The context of Bravo's story and the posthumous fate of this book is of obvious interest to this journal as a resource and perspective on the Beatles, their impact and cultural value. Christine Feldman-Barrett (2021: 50) identifies Bravo as one of the 'Apple Scruffs', the name given to an original and select group of largely female Beatles fans. They were a fixture outside Abbey Road studios — at least when band members were recording — a representative delegation of the audience that was left behind when live performances and touring were abandoned in 1966. This is a group of fans that has been imagined in Beatles mythology, notably by the band itself in the song 'She Came in through the Bathroom Window' from *Abbey Road*, and in Harrison's solo 'Apple Scruffs' from *All Things Must Pass*. They flit in and out of Beatles biographies as snapshots (e.g. Norman 2016; Shapiro 2002). More substantively, and predating Bravo, fellow Scruff Carol Bedford wrote her own memoir of the group with *Waiting for the Beatles* (1984), contributing to a wider genre of Beatles fan writing including Mitchell and Munn's *All Our Loving: A Beatles Fan's Memoirs* (1988), the eponymous Mary Mack Conger, *Sweet Beatle Dreams: The Diary of Mary Mack Conger* (1989), Margaret Hunt's *Yesterday: Memories of a Beatles Fan* (2015) and Janice Mitchell's *My Ticket to Ride* (2021). Fictionalized Scruffs play a part in William Shaw's police procedural *A Song From Dead Lips* (AKA *She's Leaving Home* 2013) and he has described them elsewhere as 'groupies' (2016), unreflexively deploying the fantasies of that label (see also Shapiro 2011). Lately, a website claiming to be the creation of original members of the Apple Scruffs has appeared announcing that 'we have remained silent for many years but now we want to tell our own unique story and dispel the myths and dispute any wrong information and inaccuracies' (Apple Scruffs n.d.).

The Apple Scruffs' desire to own and write their own history accords with a wider scholarly 'return' to Beatles fandom. A range of work, respectful of the varied ways in which the Beatles were experienced, seeks to understand the rich and varied ways in which audiences were constituted and developed relationships with the band (Mills 2019; Feldman-Barrett 2021; Womack and O'Toole 2021). Such work draws on websites and social media, a prodigious range of podcasts, personal archives and the appearance of the aforementioned memoirs and self-published works like those of Hunt and Bravo as well as films such as Paul Saltzman's *Meeting the Beatles in India* (2020). Such resources document the meaning of the band for fans in its original flourishing and as something that has become an enduring inter-generational inheritance.

Do Rio a Abbey Road is available in Portuguese, although Bravo has given a precis of her experience in various English-language interviews, offering a glimpse of the richness of this memoir and an appreciation of how it might appeal to readers beyond the Lusophone world. It has something to say about the devotion engendered by the Beatles, of the community of fandom and the industriousness of individuals and how they add to our comprehension of what the band was and why they endure. While this story deserves to be read in Bravo's words, aspects are worth recounting from the perspective of her daughter Marya, who is now charged with maintaining her mother's rich legacy and the dissemination of her book.

Speaking in an interview with the author in April 2022, Marya related how Bravo managed a 'kind of a trick' to get her parents to send her and a friend to London in 1967. For middle-class families at that time in Brazil, a child's fifteenth birthday was a significant marker: 'you could choose: either your family gave you a huge party or you got a trip to Europe' (Bravo 2022; see also Feldman-Barrett 2021: 75). The difference for Lizzie was 'she never came back' (Bravo 2022) – or at least she remained in London for three years, largely making her own way. The motive for going to London was, of course, the Beatles. As Marya relates, Bravo had become acquainted with the group's music when her father brought back an album for her from his travels. Then a short cinema feature on the band galvanized her friendships and 'a group formed of these girls that were in love with them and they started sharing things' (Bravo 2022). They would nurture Beatles pen pals and meet as a group to listen to records or see *A Hard Day's Night* and *Help!* at the cinema. More precisely, Marya confirms a specific motive for Bravo's pilgrimage: 'it wasn't even the Beatles, it's just John. She's in love with John [...] and she wanted to be near him and that's what drove her' (Bravo 2022). As she cautions, however, and as anatomized in *Do Rio a Abbey Road*, 'you read the diaries and it's just a 15-year-old saying how much she loves John Lennon [...] it's really very naïve, very sweet' (Bravo 2022).

On the very day she landed in London, Bravo headed straight to Abbey Road. Her friend who had journeyed ahead had identified how a band of fans had established an almost continuous presence at the studio – any absence a signal that no Beatles were at work there. On that first day, Bravo managed to see and meet all of the band members in person, creating a photographic record that she would continue to accrue over her time in attendance at the studio. She also took a souvenir from John Lennon's psychedelically decorated Rolls Royce, a glove that she wiped across it; 'it's in her collection with the dust from John's car' (Bravo 2022).

After this first visit, 'she would just see them every day', and indeed was able to *hear* them at work: 'she said back then you could hear the recordings — it wasn't so acoustic and so she heard them recording *Sergeant Pepper's*, "The White Album" and *Abbey Road*'. The memoir recounts many such details and anecdotes, 'like John arriving with his Sergeant Pepper's outfit and showing it to her saying "look: this is what we're gonna wear on the cover"' (Bravo 2022). The continual presence of the Apple Scruffs allowed for the nurturing of a particular relationship with the band: 'they weren't friends or anything. They were fans, they were treated like fans but they [the Beatles] knew their names, you know, they were always the same faces' (Bravo 2022). While holiday periods would see a swelling in numbers of fans and sightseers outside the studio, creating an echo of the days of 'Beatlemania', Bravo and other regulars became a fixture signalling a form of normalization: 'sometimes they would just hang out and talk or she would walk home with Paul. Paul lived very close so sometimes they would walk him home and things like that' (Bravo 2022). In fact, in order to aid Bravo with a language-learning project in which she was involved, McCartney insisted on lending her a tape recorder. On another occasion John and Yoko Ono asked Bravo to go and buy a birthday cake. As Marya ponders 'I think they just got more used to them' (Bravo 2022).

This proximity was what lent the obsessions of fandom a routinized quality. Bravo's documentation of her interactions with Paul and John in particular was as persistent as any press pack: 'she had this little instamatic camera it wasn't anything incredible you know she just had her little camera that she took [...] I don't know how many photos — there's so many — 600 — she was just taking photos of them all the time' (Bravo 2022). This context, then, is one in which what Marya notes is 'the most famous story' of Bravo's contribution to 'Across the Universe' can be understood as a rather casual occurrence amidst the group's everyday creative labour, even if it is framed as exceptional:

> she'd been hanging around for a while before that opportunity came up [...] they were sitting outside and [...] Paul comes out and asks if any of them knows how to hold a high note [...] and my mother had always sang in school in choir [...] the family has always been very musical and so she said she could and he said okay just a second and so she waited and you know people are freaking out like 'oh my God you're gonna go in!' And she asked if she could take a friend and she knew another one of the friends – the Apple Scruffs – that one of the other ones sang [Gayleen Pease] also, so she asked if she could take her because she was terrified, you know, sixteen, going inside the studio with the Beatles. It's pretty amazing and they spent like four hours or something in the studio with them and now she's on the record. (Bravo 2022)

Marya has pondered the daunting nature of this event and her mother's mission by way of comparison with her own life as a musician, recalling how: 'I left home when I was seventeen but I went with the job. I went with a tour and I was really young but [...] I had some sort of structure; you know, it was pretty crazy but I keep thinking about it. I think of her – fifteen years old just going to another completely different culture and it was really, really, brave' (Bravo 2022). While a life of relative privilege had enabled Bravo to travel to London, once there she had to sustain herself over three expatriate years. As her daughter comments, at home her life was made comfortable by the support of domestic servants, 'and she had never made her own bed', whereas in London, 'she arrived there and she just went to work as a hotel cleaning woman' (Bravo 2022). On the other hand, such work meant one could be relatively free to spend hours outside Abbey Road studios. This involved some dedication: 'She was in London for three years: she's working, she's studying English, but most days she's dedicating herself to going hanging out at the Beatles studio [...] she talks a lot about how cold it was sometimes [...] about the police coming and "shooing them", telling them to leave and there were a lot of uh hard, hard moments like that' (Bravo 2022).

Ultimately, Bravo and the other Scruffs ended their observance at Abbey Road when the Beatles' work practices and relationships with each other fractured: 'they weren't going to the studios every day anymore, it wasn't like before' (Bravo 2022). Bravo had also grown up a little and 'I think she kind of wanted you know to go get on with her life [...] so I think that's what made her come back' (Bravo 2022). Returning to Brazil and establishing herself as a professional singer and photographer, Bravo collaborated with musicians such as Milton Nascimento, Zé Ramalho and Zé Rodrix. She later married Rodrix, who paid tribute to her in his composition 'Casa no Campo' ('House in the Country').

According to Marya, her mother made little of her contribution to 'Across the Universe', talking of it as if it was an everyday occurrence. However, her passionate commitment to the Beatles and to other fans endured, manifest in her networks, communications and collection: 'she's like a good, lucky historian: she's kept all of her materials and records [...] she had two album covers signed by the four of them and she sold them a long time ago and she has a lot of autographs' (Bravo 2022). This commitment was expressed too in Bravo's decision to write a book about her experience even as she attended to her career and family: 'Since I was born, it's all I heard about was the book, the book, and she has to write the book [...] and everyone is asking her when she's gonna write the book' (Bravo 2022). The writing was a labour of forty years or more, as Marya recalls her mother commencing writing it on an old Macintosh computer in the 1980s before finalizing publication in 2015. Self-published and self-distributed, the book became an end in itself, a kind of occupation as Marya describes it, as her mother 'answered all the emails and went to the post office and sent all the books [...] she did really hard work' (Bravo 2022).

Recent excitement generated in Brazil by a teaser for a mooted biopic, a 'proof-of concept' video that went viral on social media, attests to the interest in Bravo's experience, which escaped its specificity as particular kind of fan story. As Marya relates in reflecting on the way in which the film, which is no more than an idea, generated a response: 'It wasn't related to the Beatles anymore. People really were amazed at her story: the story of a girl going to London by herself to follow a dream and it just really touched them' (Bravo 2022). This impacted on sales of *Do Rio A Abbey Road* 'because before that she was only selling to Beatles fans and then all of a sudden there were like people from every area and every job wanting to read her story' (Bravo 2022).

Marya ruminated on this interest and the legacy of how 'this is all mine now you know [...] I'm still trying to figure out what I'm gonna do with everything' (Bravo 2022). Aside from questions about the status of Bravo's personal archive, and the interest in making the film or TV series based on this story, the objective is to obtain an international publisher for the book in the Anglophone world and beyond. To this end, Marya has been working with US entertainment lawyer Joel H. Weinstein. Originally commissioned by Bravo, an English translation already exists although key issues concern the form in which any further publication appears and the respect accorded to her intentions. She was particular about the design and presentation of the book, as she wrote on her website: 'I chose to make the book independently, exactly as I imagined it, with creative freedom' (lizziebravo.com). As Marya says of publishers who were originally interested in the book, 'I guess they always want to meddle, edit and change' (Bravo 2022). That is the challenge for any future publication: how to maintain the integrity and personal touch of Bravo's creation. 'That's something that I'm gonna have to work with within myself you know because I believe that she wanted to keep self-publishing the English version also, but I have no way of doing that as it's really a full-time job' (Bravo 2022). She conveys also the intensely personal challenge of her role, of how 'when you have a parent who is like a public person you know it's really hard sometimes because you can't just be normal' (Bravo 2022). Nonetheless, 'it's beautiful how people want to show their love and they want to show how much they care' (Bravo 2022). Consequently, Marya says of her inheritance that 'I can't just keep it all to myself you know, I need to share the story' (Bravo 2022).

The context for this discussion prompts one to imagine many other such ventures of a similar nature documenting fan activities, whether invested in personal archives, diaries, memoirs, oral histories, recordings or other format. By any estimation, however, Lizzie Bravo's book represents a very particular achievement in documenting *this* girl who sang with the Beatles. It draws attention both to the value gained from being a Beatles fan but also the values generated by a lifetime's commitment to the band and indeed creating a community of interest with others in its audience. The core value of Lizzie Bravo's enterprise is expressed on her website: 'Know that this book was made with lots of love!' *A Rio Do Abbey Road* invites us to consider it in relation to the broader enterprising labour and reward of fandom, of the generation of such resources that aid us in making sense of the Beatles in their time and in terms of their legacy. The book's spirit is maintained by Marya Bravo in seeking as wide an audience as possible with which to share her mother's generous insights: 'Across the Universe' indeed!

Paul Long
Monash University, Australia
paul.long@monash.edu

Acknowledgements

My sincere thanks are extended to Marya Bravo and Joel H. Weinstein for prompting this article.

Bibliography

Apple Scruffs (n.d.) 'About Us', applescruffs.co.uk (accessed 29 June 2022).

Bedford, Carol (1984) *Waiting on the Beatles: An Apple Scruffs Story* (Poole: Blandford Press).

Bravo, Lizzie (2015) *Do Rio a Abbey Road* (self-published).

Bravo, Lizzie (n.d.) lizziebravo.com (accessed 29 June 2022).

Bravo, Marya (2022) Interview with author, 14 April 2022.

Conger, Mary Mack (1989) *Sweet Beatle Dreams: The Diary of Mary Mack Conger* (Kansas City: Andrews McMeel Publishing).

Feldman-Barrett, Christine (2021) *A Women's History of the Beatles* (New York: Bloomsbury).

Hemenway, Robert [Stephen Patch] (1969) 'The Girl Who Sang with the Beatles', *New Yorker*, 3 January 1969: 26–33.

Hopkins, Jerry, John Burks and Paul Nelson (1969) 'The groupies and other girls from the Plaster Casters to the GTOs and Trixie Merkin, an investigation into female band groupies', *Rolling Stone*, 15 February 1969, https://www.rollingstone.com/feature/groupies-gtos-miss-mercy-plaster-caster-75990/ (accessed 29 June 2022).

Hunt, Margaret (2015) *Yesterday: Memories of a Beatles Fan* (Self-published: Kindle edition).

Mills, Richard (2019) *The Beatles and Fandom: Sex, Death and Progressive Nostalgia* (New York: Bloomsbury).

Mitchell, Carolyn Lee and Michael Munn (1988) *All Our Loving: A Beatles Fan's Memoirs* (London: Robson Books).

Mitchell, Janice (2021) *My Ticket to Ride: How I Ran Away to England to Meet the Beatles and Got Rock and Roll Banned in Cleveland (a True Story from 1964)* (Cleveland: Gray).

Norman, Philip (2016) *Paul McCartney: The Life* (London: Weidenfeld and Nicolson).

Saltzman, Paul (dir.) (2020) *Meeting the Beatles in India*.

Shapiro, Marc (2002) *All Things Must Pass: The Life of George Harrison* (London: Virgin).

Shaw, William (2013) *A Song from Dead Lips* (London: Quercus).

Shaw, William (2016) 'The Beatles and the Apple Scruffs', 20 February 2016, http://williamshaw.com/the-beatles-and-the-apple-scruffs/ (accessed 29 June 2022).

Womack, Kenneth and Kit O'Toole (eds) (2021) *Fandom and the Beatles: The Act You've Known for All These Years* (New York: Oxford University Press).

80 at 80

Commemorating Paul McCartney's eightieth birthday

Holly Tessler

Exactly one week after his eightieth birthday, Paul McCartney was the headline act at Glastonbury, performing a nearly three-hour hit-filled set in front of a live audience of around 100,000, plus millions more watching on television. There is perhaps no other pop music performer today with a larger and more robust catalogue of songs from which to draw or with a larger fan base of ecstatic followers singing along with every word.

As part of the pre-Glasto festivities, Paul's social media team invited fans to create their 'dream set list' drawn from a list of fifty songs spanning the whole of his career (Universal Music 2022). It is an idea that we, the editorial board of the *Journal of Beatles Studies*, adapted into what we believe is a fitting way of commemorating Paul on the occasion of his eightieth birthday. Limiting ourselves to just twenty songs each, collectively we have created an '80 at 80 list' of tracks written by Paul McCartney that are significant to each of us. As anyone who has attempted to compile a (play)list like this can attest, choosing just a handful of favourite Paul songs is a near-impossibility. As my colleagues have noted elsewhere, our lists, individually and cooperatively, should not be considered definitive in either critical or personal contexts. Instead, our lists reflect our thinking about why, how and what about Paul McCartney's words and music resonate with us at this point in our lives. We have added our

The Journal of Beatles Studies Autumn (2022)

ISSN 2754-7019 (online)

https://doi.org/10.3828/jbs.2022.8

selections into a Spotify playlist that you can find on the Spotify website.[1]

As you'll see, each of the four of us has come at this task in a markedly different way, which in itself is reflective of the wider complexities of popular music fandom and the nuances of affect (Duffett 2015; Long et al. 2017). For me, trying to assemble anything like a shortlist of favourite Paul songs proved a hopeless task. Instead, I started from a point of thinking not about individual songs but rather of the qualities embodied in Paul's music that are meaningful to me. From there, I selected tracks that I felt are good examples of those qualities. Thus, I have less of a 'top 20' than a set of songs loosely coalescing around four very broad concepts. Like my colleagues, I have avoided using an overarching 'countdown' narrative structure.

The 'lost' recordings

Paul, like John Lennon, was adept at absorbing the aesthetic influences around him. In the earliest days of his songwriting career, Paul's influences were plainly evident in the songs he wrote:

> For me, the first thing was to copy other people, like Buddy Holly and Little Richard — and Elvis, who, I later heard, didn't even write his own songs. It meant memorising their songs, learning the standards of early rock and roll, but in my early to mid-teens it occurred to me to try writing my own. I'd start off with the very simplest idea, and I'd see what came out ... Even as early as 1956 ... a musical direction was emerging: you can hear that the chord sequence descends, and the melody or the vocal ascends. I'm already playing with little musical things, very simple things, which fascinated me even though I did not know quite what they were. (McCartney 2021: xii)

Accordingly, the songs I've placed in this category are ones never officially released by Paul or the Beatles at the time they were

---

1. Scan the QR code or, alternatively, copy the url into a browser: https://open.spotify.com/playlist/7MCcTnkGcVKgABBSygo76e.

recorded. To use Paul's word, they are examples of an *emerging* musical expression. Retrospectively, these songs allow listeners a kind of behind-the-scenes glimpse into Paul's early creative process as he developed the sound that would define the songwriter and performer he would soon become.

1. 'In Spite of All the Danger' (1958). An evident homage to Elvis Presley's 'Tryin' to Get Back to You' (Everett 2001: 26; Lewisohn 2013: 171), this early and rare McCartney—Harrison collaboration illustrates how influential Presley was on what was to become the 'Beatle sound'.

2. 'I'll Be on My Way' (1963). A lovely example of Paul (and John's) admiration of Buddy Holly chord progressions and Everly Brothers harmonies. Yet it is one of the many McCartney tracks deemed by the Beatles not good enough for the group to release themselves. The fact that it reached number 2 in the U.K. pop charts for Billy J. Kramer & The Dakotas in 1963 evidences how even one of Paul's 'throwaway' songs still proved its potential for commercial success.

3. 'That Means a Lot' (1965). Another 'throwaway' song by Paul that went on to be a hit for another pop act, in this case P.J. Proby. With echoes of other moody pop hits of the age such as Gerry & The Pacemakers' 'Don't Let the Sun Catch You Crying' and Petula Clark's 'Downtown', 'That Means a Lot' illustrates McCartney's awareness of and ear for the work of other contemporary pop singers and songwriters of the period.

4. 'Step Inside Love/Los Paranoias' (1968). Whilst there are many other versions of both these tracks, I'm drawn to this particular recording (taken from *Anthology 3*) because it gives us a glimpse into Paul's creative process, eavesdropping on a work-in-progress that would become the hit theme song to Cilla Black's television programme. But its collapse into the ad hoc improv jam of 'Los Paranoias' affords the listener a rare opportunity to hear the spontaneity, humour and sheer creative chemistry shared between McCartney and Lennon.

The 'Beatlesque'

Writing in 1996, Timothy Scheurer (1996: 89) observed that 'If any of us had even $10 for each time we have read the term "Beatlesque" or have read how the Beatles have influenced a musical group or performer since 1970, we might all have a tidy nest egg for our retirement'. In seeking to apply a more precise definition of the term, he observed that 'Beatlesque' music broadly references the Beatles' compositional use of harmonies and 'catchy melodies' (1996: 95), the musicological specifics of which he details at length. But for non-musicologist Beatles fans, we simply know 'the Beatle sound' when we hear it. And it is largely Paul's mid-Beatles period of increasingly intricate songwriting and lyrical introspection that really edified the sound and emotion that 'Beatlesque' musicians have aspired to ever since (see Feldman-Barrett 2021).

5. 'I've Just Seen a Face' (1965). An example of McCartney's evolution towards a more mature and folk rock-influenced style, the 'jingly-jangly' acoustic sound of this track helped to definitively move the Beatles beyond their 'moptop' period.

6. 'We Can Work It Out' (1965). Eminently 'sing-alongable', the lyrics of this well-known middle-period Beatles track reflect the near-universal experience of trying to salvage a relationship destined to 'fall apart before too long'.

7. 'Paperback Writer' (1966). A prime example of one of McCartney's 'story songs', evidencing his growing confidence and sophistication in musical and lyrical composition.

8. 'Hello, Goodbye' (1967). McCartney's trademark mix of optimism and wistfulness. One of the most quintessentially 'Beatlesque' songs there is.

9. 'Penny Lane' (1967). Like 'Hello, Goodbye', McCartney's blend of cheerfulness tinged with nostalgia is reflected melodically and lyrically in a song about different kinds of trips: physical, imagined, psychedelic.

10. 'Getting Better' (1967). Described by John Lennon as a 'pure Beatle' song (Miles 1969: 33).

11. 'Calico Skies' (1997). McCartney's own reinterpretation of the 'Beatlesque' decades later.

Live performance

As critic Marv Watson (2022) observed of Paul's most recent U.S. tour:

> The crowd of all ages (there's a group of 20-somethings just ahead of this reviewer, singing along to EVERY WORD, not just Beatles-era) is hugely engrossed in the whole spectacle, and aside from the usual 'film every note' types in the audience, everyone is engaged and present. McCartney plays for over two and a half hours, incredible for anyone regardless of age, and he barely looks like he's broken a sweat. The songs were played to perfection, another testament to just *how* good he is. How good he's always been.

Limiting discussion of Paul's music 'only' to his compositions and recordings would miss out the fact that when performed live, many of McCartney's songs, to use the vernacular of the moment, just hit different, creating multisensory, emotionally impactful experiences.

12. 'Maybe I'm Amazed' (1970). The live version of this song, which, in recent tours, has been accompanied by video footage of Paul's late wife, Linda, and then-infant daughter, Mary, snuggled in his coat (the image which would become the cover of his first solo album, *McCartney*), creates a genuinely poignant moment for performer and audience alike.

13. 'Live and Let Die' (1973). The (literally) incendiary show-stopper of any McCartney gig. Perhaps no one has more aptly described the experience than Paul himself:

> It's still a big show tune for us to this day. We have pyrotechnics, and the thing I think I like most about it is that we know the explosion's

about to happen, that big first explosion. Often I look at the people, particularly in the front row, who are blithely going along, 'Live and let...' BOOM! It's great to watch them; they're shocked. One night I noticed a very old woman in the front row, and I thought, 'Oh shit, we're going to kill her.' But there was no stopping, I couldn't stop the song and say, 'Cover your ears, love!' So when it came to that line, I looked away. 'Live and let...' BOOM! And I looked back at her, and she hadn't died after all. She was grinning from ear to ear and loving it. (2021: 428)

14. 'Hey Jude' (1968). Not only the ultimate sing-along moment of any live gig, McCartney or otherwise, but also the ultimate sing-along moment of any late-night train journey in Liverpool on a Saturday night.

Production techniques and alternative versions

A grouping intended to serve as a very rough kind of counterpoint to McCartney's Beatlesque songs, the tracks listed here are those where the performance rather than the composition are foregrounded. With added layers of orchestration, or stripped back and reinterpreted, these songs, for me, spotlight McCartney's abilities and instincts as a producer, arranger and musical director, foreshadowing his later work in the electronica and classical genres.

15. 'Helter Skelter' (1968). I never really paid much attention to 'Helter Skelter' until I heard Giles Martin's breathtaking remaster of *The Beatles* album in 2018. A radical departure from the more contemplative and melodic 'Beatlesque' period, McCartney deliberately wrote this song to 'try to make the meters peak' (McCartney 2021: 265). Particularly when listened to with headphones, it is a dizzying sonic spectacle of a recording.

16. 'Nineteen Hundred and Eighty Five' (1974). A younger sibling of 'Live and Let Die', this banger of a track, replete with sci-fi synths and an explosive, pyrotechnic orchestral ending is the thundering, triumphant climax to *Band on the Run*.

17. 'Coming Up' (1980). With a killer hook and horn section, a track that, with the exception of some vocal harmonies by Linda, was written, performed, recorded and produced entirely by Paul McCartney alone.

18. 'Rockestra Theme' (1979). One of McCartney's most overlooked instrumental compositions, it serves as the *de facto* theme song to Wings' *Back To The Egg* album. But I primarily make reference here to the video version of this track, as captured live in the *Concert for The People of Kampuchea* film (dir. Keith McMillan, 1980), featuring a windmilling Pete Townshend, showboat-y and lairy in equal measure, the only member of the 'Rockestra' not wearing a silver-sequined jacket.

19. 'Take It Away' (1982). Another moment of pop perfection punctuated by another killer hook and horn section.

20. 'Every Night' (1992; from *Unplugged: The Official Bootleg*). Unlike the other songs in this group, this version of 'Every Night' is not lavishly orchestrated or produced, but rather stripped down and acoustic, as was the fad in the early 1990s. But in doing so, McCartney produces a soulful and nuanced performance that elevates it far beyond the original studio recording.

Holly Tessler
University of Liverpool, UK
Holly.Tessler@liverpool.ac.uk

Bibliography

Duffett, Mark (2016) *Popular Music Fandom* (Abingdon: Routledge).

Everett, Walter (2001) *The Beatles as Musicians: The Quarry Men through Rubber Soul* (Oxford: Oxford University Press).

Feldman-Barrett, Christine (2021) *A Women's History of the Beatles* (London: Bloomsbury).

Lewisohn, Mark (2013) *The Beatles: All These Years, Volume One: Tune In* (New York: Crown Archetype).

Long, Paul, Sarah Baker, Lauren Istvandity and Jez Collins (2017) 'A labour of love: the affective archives of popular music culture', *Archives and Records* 38(1): 61–79.

McCartney, Paul (2021) *The Lyrics*, 2 vols, ed. Paul Muldoon (London: Allen Lane).

Miles, Barry (1969) '*Abbey Road:* The Beatles come together', *Oz* [London], November 1969, 32–33, https://archivesonline.uow.edu.au/nodes/view/4848#idx26959 (accessed 7 September 2022).

Scheurer, Timothy E. (1996) 'The Beatles, the Brill Building, and the persistence of Tin Pan Alley in the age of rock', *Popular Music and Society* 20(4): 89–102.

Universal Music (2022) Create Your Dream Paul McCartney Set List [website], https://live.umusic.com/paulmccartney (accessed 25 June 2022).

Watson, Marv (2022) 'Live review: Paul McCartney live In Los Angeles', mxdwn.com, 16 May 2022, https://music.mxdwn.com/2022/05/16/reviews/live-review-paul-mccartney-live-in-los-angeles/ (accessed 25 June 2022).

Paul Long

Literary scholar F.R. Leavis opened *The Great Tradition* with the announcement that 'The great English novelists are Jane Austen, George Eliot, Henry James and Joseph Conrad' (1948: 1), determining this to be a safe point to stop in his listing. Scholars and cultural intermediaries across the arts have long been involved in such active canon formation, even if the confident entitlement of such assertions is subject to challenge and deconstruction (Guillory 1993; Sela-Sheffy 2002). Of course, canons, best-of (and worst-of) lists, as well as charts of sale and popularity are an integral part of how the music industry and its vernacular cultures are constituted (Kärjä 2006). There's joy in thinking about and sharing what we value and why we value popular music but also for its status alongside the authorization of more rarefied cultural forms such as the English novel.

Whatever the field, one's preferred artists and texts, and our evaluation of them, are things that serve as forms of social distinction, signalling one's tastes, affiliations and indeed identity (Bourdieu 1984; Kruse 1993). Some may lack the language of the academic and professional critic but still share the activity of close reading, expert knowledge and authenticity of response to the works we value (and even dislike).

A recognition of these qualities is part of the impulse of the *Journal of Beatles Studies* which, by happy accident, publishes its inaugural edition close to the occasion of Paul McCartney's eightieth birthday. Still recording and performing, he continues to draw critical attention. Whether or not apparently overshadowed by Beatles output, the romantic expectations of rock culture or even just the process of ageing, much more respect is now devoted to his post-Beatles oeuvre, including a recognition of the contexts and terms on which that work has been received.

At this moment, canon formation and evaluative lists dedicated to McCartney's works abound; authorized, formal or informal, they draw from a rich repertoire. Inevitably then, when invited to itemize a favourite twenty tracks, one is struck by one's own familiarity and ignorance. Prose presentations of musical lists and analyses have particular conventions, often itemizing details of recording and release – B-sides, album tracks, outtakes, bootleg versions of concerts attended by the writer, and so on. Sometimes lists integrate snippets of biography, anecdote and gossip. The list that follows details some thoughts about each song and why it is interesting to me *in this moment*. Absences are not oversights, nor do they imply judgements; rather these are selected because I've been listening to them of late – as an abiding practice or anew. I listen because they give me pleasure and thus present them with only the hierarchy of alphabetical order.

1. 'Another Day' (1971). A delicately detailed song that expresses an appreciation of the challenges of everyday existence measured in the banal routines of a lonely protagonist akin to those of 'Eleanor Rigby'. Songs like this one counter accusations that McCartney's work is somehow lightweight in form and content,

mistaking its melodic and tuneful affect as at odds with its subject matter. This everyday tragedy is one in which the protagonist yearns for 'the man of her dreams', yet when he 'comes to break the spell' he does not hang around. Perhaps he is only imagined, but at least the performance offers a space of empathy, optimism and thus hope about what another day might eventually bring.

2. 'Bluebird' (1973). McCartney is creative in his love songs and this is as languorous and light as the imagined flight of the bird of the song's title, a flight which, after all, takes place at night-time. The nature of such songs is one perfect evocation of what it means to be in love, recognized by those who have experienced or yearn for it.

3. 'Can You Take Me Back?' (1968). This is the tune heard on *The Beatles* (also known as the *White Album*) at the end of 'Cry Baby Cry', possibly acting as prolegomenon to 'Revolution No.9'. I've always been fascinated by the suggestive snippet which was made available as a whole with the expanded re-release of the album in 2018. The song is insistent, repetitive, obsessive even – akin to a dream state, possibly a troubled one. It sits well with 'Revolution No.9' (one of those recordings that some 'aficionados' claim ruins the album of which it is part – see also 'Yellow Submarine' – and thus is always skipped. 'Father, forgive them; for they know not what they do.' *Luke 23:34*).

4. 'Come and Get It' (1970). A discovery from the *Anthology* series.

5. 'Coming Up' (1980). Funky, fun and inventive. Aside from the irresistible beat and guitar figure, this also features a return of McCartney's distinctive Beatle-era 'Ooh!' Like some other songs in this list, McCartney's voice is noticeably altered or processed, although its relative modesty in the mix disguises a rather committed and soulful straining at times. 'Coming up: like a flower' is a delightful motif. Notable too, I think, is that at the time of release, this tune was all over TV thanks in part to the entertaining video, in which McCartney appears as the entire band with Linda as several backing singers. McCartney's

multiple appearances reference Ron Mael of Sparks, Hank Marvin of The Shadows and indeed his own Hofner-bass playing Beatlemania-era self.

6. 'Cook of the House' (1976). One might argue that this is actually Linda's song as she co-wrote it and sings it. It stands therefore for a number of other choices that might be *about* Linda across this list and the productive collaboration of this endlessly undervalued partnership. Critical derision towards the song is exactly why it is worth celebrating for its ramshackle, DIY quality, as if it, like the meals mentioned, has been whipped up to assuage a momentary hunger. It is also a profound assertion of the value of a controlling role in the domestic space whose references and feelings are conveyed across McCartney's work.

7. 'Every Night' (1970). Although I grew up with McCartney's solo work and Wings, I've paid closer attention to it since I obtained his first album a few years ago. This is one of those tunes that seemed already familiar from *somewhere*. A candid expression of a depressed soul who is unable to function, there is at least the redemptive power, promise and belief offered by the presence of a lover to whom the song is directed, and around whose invocation the melody soars.

8. 'Golden Slumbers' (1969). Outshone perhaps by other parts of *Abbey Road*'s long medley, the anchor for me is simply the take-off vocal performance which never fails to raise the hairs on my neck. There's a tremor when McCartney sings 'smiles awake you when you rise', where his voice sounds unstable. The power of this delivery belies the advice to 'sleep pretty darling'.

9. 'Let 'Em In' (1976). For a long time, I believed this to be a cover of Billy Paul's 1977 recording rather than vice versa. Paul's roll call of black leaders makes the title's plea one for political inclusion, social equality and cultural recognition. McCartney's original is slower and more groove-led than Paul's urgent call, couched as it is in the 'Sound of Philadelphia' strings. Ostensibly, McCartney is more domestic in tone and focus, the song opening with the sound of a doorbell. Yet alongside his roll call of

family names there are also those of 'Phil and Don' (Everly) and 'Martin Luther'. Perhaps it's the Protestant reformer, perhaps Dr King, but the recording expresses a warmth and humanity that explains its appeal for Billy Paul's purpose.

10. 'Let Me Roll It' (1973). One hears in this performance an echo of John Lennon's early 1970s style, particularly in the funereal beat of drum and bass and the discordant, frankly horrible guitar figure. However, the lyrical sentiment, melody and impassioned vocal delivery make it a real oddity, again underlining McCartney's often radical counterpoint. Effectively deployed in the film *Licorice Pizza* (dir. Paul Thomas Anderson, 2021).

11. 'Little Willow' (1997). Sleeve notes to the album *Flaming Pie* tell us that this was written on the death of Maureen Cox. I have no idea whether McCartney is any more or less empathetic than anyone else, but such songs capture his ability to *convey* that feeling like no another. For some years now there has been talk of McCartney's ageing voice, which is clearly changing his relationship with his songbook and creating new creative affordances in instances such as this song.

12. 'Magneto and Titanium Man' (1975). 'Rocky Raccoon' suggests how spoken-word parts on songs can be grating, but McCartney's nonsensical and nonsense assemblages can be effective and affecting while inviting interpretation and explanation. 'Jet' or 'Band on the Run' for instance engage and affect deeply, as popular music often does without deconstruction revealing rational sense. This song is exceptionally bonkers as it invites us to access McCartney's imaginative world.

13. 'She's a Woman' (1964). A good example of stating the obvious, the song itemizes the key things that make its subject both a dedicated and authentic lover. In many ways the vocal shriek expresses both immature, boyish anxiety and excitement at how the 'girl' of many previous Lennon–McCartney songs is supplanted by a more mature and committed partner (that continuity might be compromised by the title if not the subject of *Rubber Soul's* 'Girl'). A cack-handed ska guitar vies with a driving bass to create a great floor-filler for the hard-of-dancing.

14. 'Step Inside Love' (recorded by Cilla Black, 1968). Good, bad and indifferent, there are many cover versions of McCartney (and Lennon–McCartney) songs. Rather than being appropriated *by* an artist, some versions we know from the fact that they seem *for* another and so disassociated from their originator.

15. 'Sun is Shining' (2008). I know little of the *Fireman* project, but one of the begrudgingly acknowledged delights of the streaming algorithm is that it does occasionally cause one to stop and investigate its suggestions. There's not much more here than a McCartney appreciation of joy in the everyday, but that's a relative treasure. McCartney's work has a touch of the ordinary as opposed to offering the faint praise of 'an ordinary touch', which might undermine his ability to invigorate one's imagination and affective response to such material.

16. 'Thingumybob' (1968). Some things in McCartney's oeuvre might be dismissed as curios but are delightful discoveries and cause one to consider his versatility and commitment as an artist. Whether successful or otherwise, McCartney's creative drive is what makes such ventures of interest, all the better for resulting in such rewarding tunes. The title conjures up a wartime hit by Gracie Fields ('it's the girl that makes the thing/that drills the hole that holds the spring/that works the thing-ummy-bob that makes the engines roar'). More than just a pastiche of the style associated with Northern brass ensembles, this song for the Black Dyke Mills Band calls on the heritage evoked in other McCartney pieces such as 'Penny Lane' or 'Honey Pie'. The joy of this song and its particular form reminds one of how McCartney and the Beatles, together and individually, demonstrated new ways of being artists, indeed of how to live, albeit largely respectful of the meaningful qualities of their heritage. Ray Davies expressed it best in a contemporaneous song as: 'Preserving the old ways from being abused/Protecting the new ways for me and for you'.

17. 'Waterfalls' (1980). A rather maudlin love song, beautiful and anxiously addressing a lover to be cautious should they ever stray. Another example of McCartney's lyrical imagination, reminding us how love songs explore both feelings and *how* to feel.

18. 'We Can Work It Out' (1965). There is joy in the turn-taking by Lennon and McCartney in the recording of this song which is the acme of that conjunction of affective desperation and optimism mentioned elsewhere. The song's greatness is affirmed too in Stevie Wonder's 1970 interpretation, a superior cover version from one who understood the pitfalls of such tributes after hearing the myriad maulings afforded his own 'You Are the Sunshine of My Life'.

19. 'Wonderful Christmastime' (1980). Scrooges beware! An annual event for members of the Beatles fan club was the receipt of a dedicated Christmas record from the band that would feature them singing carols, expressing messages of thanks, performing comedy sketches and engaging in general tomfoolery. I heard these recordings from bootlegs compiled on tapes shared by friends and they expanded immeasurably my appreciation of the Beatles' universe. So, McCartney's investment in the season has a history both dedicated, creative and dutiful, and one should not overlook this song, which is probably one of those we encounter most, albeit seasonally and not always heard. It accords with that aspect of McCartney's work which chronicles and celebrates the everyday and the domestic and which illustrates his versatility rather than confirming a conservatism. Some may sniff at the apparent inauthenticity of Christmas songs in general (or McCartney exercises such as 'We All Stand Together') but good work is good work. Bah humbug!

20. 'You Won't See Me' (1965). *Rubber Soul* is such a super set in which this song might be a little overlooked, although its melody and the vocal harmonies of the band make it one I hear in my head on a daily basis.

Paul Long
Monash University, Australia
paul.long@monash.edu

Bibliography

Bourdieu, Pierre (1984) *Distinction: A Social Critique of the Judgement of Taste*, trans. Richard Nice (Cambridge, MA: Harvard University Press).

Guillory, John (1993) *Cultural Capital: The Problem of Literary Canon Formation* (Chicago: University of Chicago Press).

Kärjä, Antti-Ville (2006) 'A prescribed alternative mainstream: popular music and canon formation', *Popular Music* 25(1): 3—19.

Kruse, Hollu (1993) 'Subcultural identity in alternative music culture', *Popular Music* 12(1): 33—41.

Leavis, F.R. (1948) *The Great Tradition: George Eliot, Henry James, Joseph Conrad* (London: Chatto and Windus).

Sela-Sheffy, Rakefet (2002) 'Canon formation revisited: canon and cultural production', *Neohelicon* 29(2): 141—159.

Christine Feldman-Barrett

Long before I researched and wrote *A Women's History of the Beatles* (2021), I was intrigued with how the Beatles' primary songwriters of John Lennon and Paul McCartney included and celebrated women in many of their lyrics — whether the songs' female protagonists were imagined or drawn from their own lives. While Lennon's authorship of such songs is certainly noteworthy, I have been struck by the fact that the Lennon—McCartney compositions often attributed more so to McCartney (i.e., 'Paul Songs') are especially tuned-in to the diverse experiences of women's lives. This is evident whether he centres women in his songs or showcases his relationship to and feelings about them. Moreover, this theme in Paul McCartney's songwriting has continued throughout his lengthy and illustrious career.

In a 2001 interview with McCartney for *Billboard* magazine, American filmmaker Allison Anders' name was brought up as someone who had noticed the songwriter's tendency to showcase women in many of his songs (White 2001: 94). Writer Rob Sheffield, another long-standing observer of the Beatles and Paul McCartney, asserts the same in his 2017 book *Dreaming the Beatles*. Noted Beatles scholar Kenneth Womack has also spoken of the forward-thinking, pro-woman imagery within the Beatles' song catalogue (Pazzanese: 2019). More recently, in the newly popular space of Beatles podcasts, the innovative, women-led series *Another Kind of Mind* hosted an in-depth discussion of female protagonists in McCartney's songs (Lorde and Reynolds 2021). It has been a joy to realize that my long-standing observation of Paul McCartney's woman-positive lyrics is something shared and appreciated by others who care about the sociocultural impact of his music and its legacy.

While choosing songs to include in my Top 20, I realized I did not want to create a traditional, top-down list of individual songs. Considering the ones I had in mind, it was clear that some songs connected thematically. Moreover, it should be noted that my selections do not necessarily comprise my favourite Beatles, Wings, or solo Paul McCartney songs (which, to be frank, have changed over time). Nor is my analysis of these songs totally beholden to what has been said or written elsewhere about their meanings or narratives.

Female friends

1. 'Little Willow' (1997)

2. 'Baby's in Black' (1964)

3. 'Michelle' (1965)

'Little Willow' was written in memory of Maureen Cox, Ringo Starr's first wife, who passed away from cancer in 1994 at the age of 48. McCartney, like Starr, had known her since the early 1960s when she frequented the Beatles' shows at the Cavern Club in Liverpool (O'Toole 2012; Sheffield 2017: 2). I am hard-pressed to think of another song penned by a male songwriter whose subject is a female family friend. Since no memoir or biography was written, this is also one of the few public documents of Maureen's life, with Cox a somewhat enigmatic figure in Beatles history. Little wonder that brief-but-joyful appearance in Peter Jackson's *The Beatles: Get Back* (2021) sparked much curiosity among fans old and new. Another enigmatic presence is the woman featured in the Beatles' 1964 song 'Baby's in Black'. Some have speculated that it is a song about the band's influential Hamburg friend Astrid Kirchherr, whose engagement to original Beatles bassist Stuart Sutcliffe tragically ended with his untimely death in 1962. This suggested association between Kirchherr and the song is likely influenced by the graphic novel *Baby's in Black: Astrid Kirchherr, Stuart Sutcliffe, and The Beatles* (Bellsdorf 2014), which depicts the Kirchherr—Sutcliffe romance. Like the bohemian figure of German friend Astrid Kirchherr, the French (and fictional) 'Michelle' of the 1965 Lennon—McCartney song evokes a Left Bank love interest — potentially an acquaintance or friend who may not be fully aware of the narrator's amorous feelings. As an interesting bit of backstory to the song's composition, McCartney consulted with Jan Vaughan — a language teacher and the wife of his school friend Ivan — to help him more accurately express himself in the French lyrics (Thompson 2008: 205).

Young women

4. 'She's Leaving Home' (1967)

5. 'Another Day' (1971)

6. 'Daytime Nighttime Suffering' (1979)

7. 'Jenny Wren' (2005)

There is a body of sociological scholarship that examines young people's transition into adulthood. Not surprisingly, this literature often depicts youth to be as challenging as it is exciting. The period of adolescence through young adulthood has often been associated with G. Stanley Hall's notion of 'storm and stress' (Woodman 2017: 20), when concerns for the future loom large and one's desire for independence from parental control is fierce. Further, it has been young women who have traditionally encountered more barriers to adult freedoms (e.g., Feldman-Barrett 2021: 27). In this context, McCartney's lyrics about young womanhood in these four songs are both perceptive and thoughtful. 'She's Leaving Home', written during a decade when the number of teenage runaways seemed to increase, is sensitive to both the determined young girl in question (who was based on a real person) and her concerned parents (Staller 2006; Runtagh 2017). The later compositions 'Another Day', 'Daytime Nighttime Suffering' and 'Jenny Wren' also speak to the challenges and melancholia that may arise from women's lived experiences and the emotional labour that often comes with traditional female roles — whether as a single woman or as a wife and mother.

Mature women

8. 'Eleanor Rigby' (1966)

9. 'English Tea' (2005)

One can look at 'Eleanor Rigby' and 'English Tea' as interesting bookends to one another. I contend that 'English Tea' offers an alternative ending to the story of Eleanor Rigby — what might have become of her under different circumstances. The 1966 Lennon–McCartney song ruminates on the supposedly lonely lives of elderly, single women — an often 'invisible demographic' pushed aside in Western culture both then and now (Meagher 2014). 'English Tea', written almost forty years after 'Eleanor Rigby', presents listeners with a very different portrait of a woman's later life. The implied mature woman in the song, which I recall McCartney referring to when he performed it at Madison Square Garden in 2005, comes across as content with the life she's lived (and continues to enjoy). The character is presented as happily admiring the traditional beauty around her — whether it is taking in views of the British countryside, with its willow trees and roses, or enjoying a cheerful, chatty teatime with family and friends. However, whether cheerful or not, McCartney nonetheless *sees* and *values* the lives of older women — a perspective that remains rare in the history of rock music.

Women musicians

10. 'Love of the Loved' (1963)

11. 'Yesterday' (1965)

12. 'Goodbye' (1969)

13. 'Let It Be' (1970)

Paul McCartney has not only featured a diverse array of women in his lyrics, but also often considered women artists performing his songs while in the process of writing them. This was true in launching Cilla Black's career in 1963 with 'Love of the Loved' or when thinking that 'Yesterday', 'Goodbye' and 'Let It Be' would be songs ideally delivered by Marianne Faithfull, Mary Hopkin, and Aretha Franklin respectively (Feldman-Barrett 2021: 113–115). McCartney always seems to have cared that his songs could be easily adopted into women musicians' varied repertoires. As with most Lennon–McCartney compositions, the universality of their sentiments is also why so many women artists have covered and continue to reinterpret and reinvent Beatles songs.

Romantic co-adventurers

14. 'Hold Me Tight' (1963)

15. 'Two of Us' (1970)

16. 'The Back Seat of My Car' (1971)

The excitement and giddiness inherent in the Beatles' 'Hold Me Tight' (1963) easily evoke the thrills of young love. Little wonder it was the song selected for an early scene in Julie Taymor's Beatles-themed film *Across the Universe* (2007), which depicts both main characters' first blush with romance during the early 1960s. But the lyrical imagery of romantic adventure is more pronounced in 1970's 'Two of Us'. McCartney has said the song was written about random drives through the countryside during the late 1960s with then-girlfriend Linda Eastman (Du Noyer 2015). After they married, the McCartneys' partnership manifested musically through the recording of the 1971 album *Ram*, which is credited to both Paul and Linda, and further albums with their 1970s band Wings. The anthemic, triumphant sound of *Ram*'s 'The Back Seat of My Car' — especially given Paul and Linda's repeated singing of the fact that the song's characters 'can't be wrong' — is evocative of their bond as husband and wife and, importantly, as co-adventurers in work and play.

Girlfriends and wives

17. 'And I Love Her' (1964)

18. 'Maybe I'm Amazed' (1970)

19. 'Heather' (2001)

20. 'My Valentine' (2012)

While it is not unusual for composers to write music influenced by or dedicated to girlfriends and wives, it is not always transparent to audiences which person influenced a particular composition or song. However, with these four songs — spanning from McCartney's relationship with actress Jane Asher during the 1960s to wife Nancy Shevell, whom he married in 2011 — it is always clear for whom the song has been written. Moreover, McCartney's acknowledgement of the impact of each individual woman and their relationship on his life is, once again, fairly unusual within rock songwriting. Both 'Maybe I'm Amazed' and 'My Valentine' continue to feature regularly in McCartney's concert set list as loving tributes to wives Linda and Nancy (Wood 2022).

Christine Feldman-Barrett
Griffith University, Australia
c.barrett@griffith.edu.au

Bibliography

Bellsdorf, Arne (2014) *Baby's in Black: Astrid Kirchherr, Stuart Sutcliffe, and The Beatles* (New York: First Second Books).

Du Noyer, Paul (2015) *Conversations with McCartney* (New York: Overlook).

Feldman-Barrett, Christine (2021) *A Women's History of the Beatles* (New York: Bloomsbury).

Jackson, Peter (dir.) (2021) *The Beatles: Get Back*.

Lorde, Phoebe and Thalia Reynolds (2021) 'McCartney's Female Protagonists' [podcast], Another Kind of Mind: A Different Kind of Beatles Podcast, 10 May 2021, https://podcasts.apple.com/gb/podcast/female-protagonists-in-mccartney-songs/id1472107627?i=1000520953118 (accessed 24 June 2022).

Meagher, Michelle (2014) 'Against the invisibility of old age: Cindy Sherman, Suzy Lake, and Martha Wilson', *Feminist Studies* 40(1): 101–143.

O'Toole, Kit (2012) 'Paul McCartney "Little Willow" from *Flaming Pie* (1997): deep Beatles', *Something Else Reviews*, 21 December 2012, https://somethingelsereviews.com/2012/12/21/deep-beatles-paul-mccartney-little-willow-1997/ (accessed 24 June 2022).

Pazzanese, Christina (2019) 'Baby, you can drive my car', *The Harvard Gazette*, 10 December 2019, https://news.harvard.edu/gazette/story/2019/12/kenneth-womack-explains-why-the-beatles-were-proto-feminists/ (accessed 24 June 2022).

Runtagh, Jordan (2017) 'Beatles' "Sgt. Pepper" at 50: meet the runaway who inspired "She's Leaving Home"', *Rolling Stone*, 23 May 2017, https://www.rollingstone.com/feature/beatles-sgt-pepper-at-50-meet-the-runaway-who-inspired-shes-leaving-home-124697/ (accessed 24 June 2022).

Sheffield, Rob (2017) *Dreaming the Beatles: The Love Story of One Band and the Whole World* (New York: HarperCollins).

Staller, Karen M. (2006) *Runaways: How the Sixties Counterculture Shaped Today's Practices and Policies* (New York: Columbia University Press).

Taymor, Julie (dir.) (2007) *Across the Universe*.

Thompson, Gordon (2008) *Please Please Me: Sixties British Pop, Inside Out* (Oxford: Oxford University Press).

White, Timothy (2011) 'Paul McCartney on his not-so-silly love songs: exclusive discussion of new "Wingspan" and Beatles "1"', *Billboard*, 17 March 2001, 1, 94–97.

Wood, Mikael (2022) 'On the cusp of 80, Paul McCartney is still our most charming rock god', *LA Times*, 14 May 2022, https://www.latimes.com/entertainment-arts/music/story/2022-05-14/paul-mccartney-get-back-concert-sofi-stadium (accessed 24 June 2022).

Woodman, Dan (2017) 'The sociology of generations and youth studies', in *Routledge Handbook of Youth and Young Adulthood*, ed. Andy Furlong (New York: Routledge), 20–26.

Richard Mills

In choosing a Paul McCartney Top 20, I set myself one rule: no Beatles songs! So much has been written on his Beatles work, I decided to shine a light on his solo years instead. At eighty years of age McCartney remains a cutting-edge artist. His love of remix culture had its late blooming in the fabulous song and video of the 2021 dance track 'Find My Way', recorded with Beck, which is in turn a reworking of McCartney's original song on conventional guitar, bass and drums from *McCartney III* (2020). The progressive nostalgia of the song (a repetitive bass dance track melding with McCartney's original melody) and video (the voice of today's Paul coming from the digitally enhanced, pirouetting body of 1960s Paul) epitomizes the extent to which songs are 'reworked into something new and future orientated' (Feldman-Barrett 2021: 8). McCartney cherishes his old Beatles and Wings tracks, but loves it when they are mashed with beats and raps. Much in McCartney's work is bricolage art: his old songs are often reinvigorated with new hooks, electronica and pulsating dance rhythms: his art looks far back in order to look far forward. My list ranges from *Ram* (1971) to *McCartney III Imagined* (2021). My longest think-piece on McCartney is for the song 'Mr Bellamy', as all of McCartney's prodigious gifts coalesce in this overlooked deep cut from *Memory Almost Full*

(2005). It is a character song, a story song, a dialogue between characters, a classical score, an infectious melody, an ambivalent and idiosyncratic theme. The plot is unclear, which only adds to the song's enigma. 'Mr Bellamy' encapsulates all that is aesthetically daring and audacious in McCartney's oeuvre.

1. 'Live and Let Die' (1973). After the Beatles' break-up and especially after Lennon's death, McCartney was stereotyped as the sentimentalist, the balladeer and the writer of *schlager* pop songs. Philip Norman's *Shout!* (1981) along with John Lennon's interview with Jann Wenner for *Rolling Stone* (1971), enshrined and codified Lennon as the edgy and robust artist, while McCartney was pigeon-holed as a shallow and slick craftsman. 'Live and Let Die' eschews this soft-hearted image of Paul with vigour, intensity and power. It is such an irresistible mélange of reggae, rock and melody that it has been the centrepiece of McCartney's live shows for thirty years. The pyrotechnics that accompany the song in Paul's live shows are fitting for a magnum opus that was both a Bond song and a song fervently covered by Guns N' Roses in 1991.

2. 'Band on the Run' (1974). A beautifully produced and bona fide Paul McCartney classic. With its three different parts (folk, rock, funk) it shouldn't work but nevertheless coheres perfectly. The song, with its theme of escape, was aptly recorded in Lagos, Nigeria and AIR Studios in London by Paul and Linda McCartney and Denny Laine. It is one of McCartney's longest solo songs at 5.09. 'Band on the Run' has no chorus, but still manages to be catchy and memorable. The expansive and optimistic tone of the song fits with its theme of escape perfectly. Tom Doyle writes that the tone of the song 'is one of claustrophobia, of people trapped. Then, once the breakout occurs and the chiming acoustic guitar kicks in, the fugitives sprint into the sunlight, never to return' (Doyle 2013: 123). The whole tripartite piece is an exercise in wistful blue-sky thinking!

3. 'The Back Seat of My Car' (1971). Like 'Band on the Run', 'The Back Seat of my Car' is a piano-driven McCartney song on the theme of escape. The narrative follows two star-crossed lovers and the blossoming of their romantic love despite parental disapproval. The lush instrumentation is a *tour de force*. The different song pieces come together to form a beautiful mosaic. McCartney can be heard playing an early version of the song in Peter Jackson's *Get Back* (2021). Even in this nascent version it is clear that this is a sweeping classic that could have found a good home on the *Abbey Road* medley, but as McCartney had an overabundance of classic songs, he instead held it back for his *Ram* (1971) album.

4. 'Calico Skies' (1997). A fingerpicking folk ballad in the style of the *White Album*'s 'Blackbird'. The song's refrain is as romantic and heart-breaking as anything he ever wrote: 'I will hold you for as long as you like/I'll hold you for the rest of my life'. 'Calico Skies' can be compared to 'Blackbird' and does not come off second best.

5. 'Little Lamb Dragonfly' (1973). A captivating and winsome McCartney ballad with strange imagist wordplay. A lamb and a dragonfly are juxtaposed because of their fragility. The first section of the song is in plaintive D major and C major and then transitions into a sad E major in the middle. Reputedly the song was written at Paul's Mull of Kintyre farmhouse when a local farmer gave Paul a dying lamb to nurse. The melody demonstrates McCartney's ability to convey deep sadness in such an exquisite manner.

6. 'Distractions' (1989). An overlooked classic McCartney ballad from *Flowers in the Dirt* (1998). A melancholy, haunting, circuitous rhythm and lyric about obsessive love. The album cover depicts colourful foliage being swept away on an eddying stream of viscous brown mud; the juxtaposition of beauty and ugliness a fitting metaphor for the disquieting lyrics of this song.

7. 'Waterfalls' (1980). A minimalist piece on electric piano, 'Waterfalls' is a song on McCartney's 1980 solo album *McCartney* but it is a melodic ballad that would be at home on any McCartney/Beatles album. It was released as a single on 13 June 1980 with 'Check My Machine' on the B-side. The song is a result of a Paul McCartney experiment, which was to record an album at home using mainly synthesizers. In 1979, with Wings gradually disintegrating, McCartney sat alone at home in his farmhouse in East Sussex with the latest cutting-edge equipment: synthesizers, sequencers and a Studer 16-track tape machine. McCartney played all the instruments on the album and the result was an experimental piece that he didn't intend for general release; he was only going to play it to friends. When he did just that, he was told 'that is your next album' (Rice and McCartney 1980).

8. 'Single Pigeon' (1973). A piano-song combined with a lyric of marital strife. The 'Single Pigeon' of the title is a solitary bird beneath the suburban slate-grey skies of Regent's Park. What is it with McCartney and birds? Bluebird, Blackbird, Jenny Wren, On the Wings of a Nightingale, Two Magpies, Long-Tailed Winter Bird... McCartney was a keen birdwatcher as a boy and still birdwatches between shows, and of course, he was in a band called Wings.

9. 'English Tea' (2005). McCartney's career has demonstrated that he is very adept at Baroque pop. Alan Civil's horns on 'For No One' and Dave Mason's piccolo trumpet on 'Penny Lane' show how classic arrangements have given his songs a gilded sheen. The cello and violin introduction to 'English Tea', combined with the catchy piano, show that musically it would not be out of place on the *White Album* or *Revolver*. McCartney sums up this optimistic paean to the English landscape as 'Very twee, very me!' (The Paul McCartney Project 2021).

10. 'Tomorrow' (1971). A classic from the *Wild Life* (1971) album, the song never got the attention McCartney thought it deserved. When 1970s teen idol David Cassidy recorded the song in 1976, which was produced by Bruce Johnson and Carl Wilson of the Beach Boys, much to McCartney's pleasure it finally did get its day in the sun, which was well deserved as 'Tomorrow' had the potential to be another 'Yesterday'.

11. 'Mr. Bellamy' (2007). A song from McCartney's 2007 album *Memory Almost Full*, the titular Mr Bellamy is on top of a building and won't come down. The instrumentation to the song is built around and punctuates the vocal lines: 'I'm not coming down / No matter what you do / I like it up here / without you'. This is answered by his rescuers: 'Alright Mr Bellamy: We'll have you down soon.'

McCartney's fans often read obsessive meanings into his songs and this one is particularly ripe for scrutiny. McCartney almost certainly didn't intend the song to be a reference to his ex-wife Heather Mills. However, some fans are fascinated that the title 'Mr. Bellamy', if spelled out fully as 'Mister Bellamy', is an anagram of 'Mills betray me'. In addition, lines such as 'Don't tell me what to do' and 'Don't hold my hand' have also led fans to speculate that the song could refer to his ex-wife. Indeed, McCartney fans have come up with many eccentric but always entertaining interpretations of this song. There are online posts, for instance, suggesting that Mr Bellamy is a cat that is being rescued. Others have speculated that Mr Bellamy is high on LSD and, in his delusionary state, feels that 'he's got a job to do', as if on some acid-fuelled mission nobody understands apart from himself. Part of the fun of fandom is to read one's own interpretation into songs. I like to think that two famous Mr Bellamys could have had an influence on the song: Peter Franklin Bellamy, who was an English folk singer whose work McCartney would have been aware of, and who committed suicide in 1991; and the other famous Mr Bellamy: a painting by American pop artist Roy Lichtenstein from 1961.

Such fanciful interpretation speaks to the fact the song and lyrics are composed in the way the libretto of a light opera might be, as it has a character and tells a story. The panic of the crowd is at odds with the calm felt by Mr Bellamy as he contemplates suicide. The beautiful melody describes Mr Bellamy's serenity and the sharp piano speaks to the rescuers' panic. The song is also very reminiscent of musical theatre as the melody line of the piano segues into an atmospheric elliptical section which captures the sense of terror in the onlookers, mixing mock-classical piano, baritone voices, woodwinds and a gorgeous melody. This is the work of an artist who is at home with classical composition as much as he is with the usual palette of rock instruments such as drums, bass and guitar.

In my view, 'Mr. Bellamy' ranks as one of McCartney's best character songs, easily floating up into the rarefied air of 'Eleanor Rigby', 'Lovely Rita', 'Maxwell's Silver Hammer' and 'Rocky Raccoon'. This song would not be out of place on the *White Album* and sits at the top table with the best Beatles songs. The piano riff would be enough on its own to make this track unforgettable, but we have McCartney effortlessly moving from the voice of the police to Mr Bellamy. This and 'Magneto and Titanium Man' are the only examples of characters speaking to each other in his songs.

The piano and guitar capture Mr Bellamy's character in a manner similar to Prokofiev's *Peter and the Wolf*. I can give no higher praise than that! The presenter Iain Lee has pointed out that he loves McCartney's ageing voice as it lends the narrative a warm gravitas which is at odds with the song's whimsy. Mr Bellamy is a contemporary Bartleby the Scrivener who 'Would prefer not to', happily perching above the crowd and not coming down.

12. 'Frank Sinatra's Party' (2019). A surreal bonus song from the *Travellers'* and *Explorers'* editions of *Egypt Station* (2018) which namechecks Dean Martin, Frank Sinatra and Angie Dickinson. Originally titled 'Reggae Moon/Frank Sinatra's Party', the melody comes from a demo entitled the 'Fishy Matters Underwater'

recorded in 1976. The bass line does indeed sound like bubbles floating to the surface. The lyrical refrain 'I'm undercover, but plenty of others are already flying high' is the *beau idéal* of the reggae beat. The music of this track shows McCartney's nascent interest in Techno. Ian Peel writes that 'Fishy Matters Underwater' was the result of McCartney 'messing about with Moog synthesizers, combining them with the beats of his early drum machine purchases' (Peel 2002: 77). The song is a dance groove that is the ideal sound for a club; the compressed brass in the second half of the song sounds like a guitar and McCartney repeats the line 'Fee, fi, fo, fum/I'm not the only Englishman' and changes the pronunciation of 'Englishman' to 'Englishmun' giving the lyrics a 'Rastamun' feel.

13. 'Friends To Go' (2005). 'Friends To Go' is a song written for McCartney's *Chaos and Creation in the Backyard* (2005) album. Written three years after George Harrison's death, McCartney has said that it sounds like a song George could have written. One of the stranger compositions in the McCartney canon, there is a line in which Paul communes with his dead friend, with George telling Paul, 'I've been waiting on the other side for your friends to leave so I don't have to hide'. I love this song because of the unusual subject matter. Several of McCartney's songs have been inspired by dreams of lost loved ones, most notably his 'Mother Mary', Patricia Mohin-McCartney in 'Let it Be'. A psychoanalytical reading of Paul's songs would suggest that he deals with bereavement first through dreaming and then through songwriting. Paul has recently said on *The Late Show with Stephen Colbert* (2019) that he often dreams of singing with John Lennon, and John, of course, has turned up in lyrical allusions in two McCartney songs, 'Here Today' and 'Tug of War'.

14. 'On the Wings of a Nightingale' (1984). A simple four-chord country tune based on the repetition of E A D F minor. McCartney wrote this tune for his heroes Don and Phil Everly. Don and Phil's voices meld beautifully on this track. The Everly Brothers were such an influence on the young Lennon and McCartney that on

23 April 1960 John and Paul played a sleepy Berkshire pub, The Fox and Hounds, as The Nerk Twins, modelling themselves on their idols Don and Phil. Definitely a McCartney Top 20 song, even though he didn't sing it.

15. 'This Never Happened Before' (2005). 'This Never Happened Before' is a song from *Chaos and Creation in the Backyard* (2005). On this track Paul's voice is deeper, bluesy, sadder, older. As usual, Paul's bass part is spectacular, sounding like the lead instrument, accompanied by a sparse piano and terse vocals. 'This Never Happened Before' is a superb melody: a signpost to the mature McCartney we eventually hear on *McCartney III* (2020) particularly on the track 'Women and Wives', which has a distinctly Leadbelly feel to the vocals.

16. 'Getting Closer' (1979). In 1977 McCartney toyed with the idea of releasing a punk song. Tom Doyle writes that 'At Abbey Road, on his return from the Caribbean, McCartney even knocked off a comedy punk song [...] entitled "Boil Crisis"'. McCartney revealed to the journalist the opening lines of the mickey-taking lyric: 'One night in the life of Sid, he scored with a broad in a pyramid' (Doyle 2013: 210). 'Getting Closer' from the critically lambasted *Back to the Egg* (1979) album was recorded in this punky spirit; it sounds like the power pop of Blondie and Squeeze: fast New Wave rock combined with McCartney melody. The B-side of 'Getting Closer' is 'Spin on It', which is also a fast, punchy pop song. There are superb ballads on *Back to the Egg*, such as 'Arrow Through Me', but it is McCartney acting as a conduit for the punk/New Wave zeitgeist that makes it such a memorable album, especially the ludicrously infectious 'Getting Closer'. Also, it is impossible not to love a song which rhymes 'salamander' with 'oh no, don't answer'.

17. 'Back in Brazil' (2019). 'Back in Brazil' is another in a long line of McCartney's narrative songs. The critic Sheila Whiteley refers to McCartney's 'dime store novel' approach to songwriting, pointing out that the 1960s 'counterculture was male dominated [...] and embodied the patriarchal imaginary of the Madonna—whore

binary' (Whiteley 2000: 41). This may be an accurate description of some 1960s rock music, for instance Rolling Stones songs such as 'She's a Rainbow' and 'Stupid Girl', but it clearly isn't true of McCartney. Paul's story songs are full of strong female characters: Molly Jones, Lady Madonna, Eleanor Rigby. 'Back in Brazil' continues this theme, with a strong twenty-first-century character who gets her boyfriend 'to fit in with her plan' to bring her to a Paul McCartney concert. And like Molly and Desmond they live happily ever after. A joyful party tune on which McCartney played nine instruments.

18. 'Riding to Vanity Fair' (2005). A slow-tempoed, foreboding song on glockenspiel, string section, harp and lead guitar. It has a hypnotic, mellow groove that draws me into a trance — a McCartney song full of anger, hurt and pessimism after his divorce from Heather Mills. McCartney's work with Radiohead producer Nigel Godrich during the recording of this track, which is from the album *Chaos and Creation in the Backyard,* also imbues the song with foreboding and tension.

19. 'Darkroom' (1980). The album *McCartney II* (1980) saw Paul embracing electronic, experimental, crepuscular and haunting dance music. 'Darkroom' is the creepiest song on *McCartney II.* Where cheerier tracks such as 'Coming Up', 'Check My Machine' and 'Bogey Music' gave McCartney a chance to break away from the standard bass, drums and guitars instrumentation of the typical rock band, 'Darkroom' blends synthesizers, reverb units, samples, loops and echo units with a high falsetto vocal, and treats listeners to threatening, scary, unsettling and avant-garde music you can dance to. 'Darkroom' and 'Check My Machine' are two of Paul's best dance tracks. Reviews in 1980 were bad, but this fantastic track and album have been rehabilitated by artists such as Hot Chip: 'I grew up listening to "Check My Machine" and generally dancing round the living room to it as a four- or five-year-old. I still listen a lot to the album now — it is one of my all-time favourites' (quoted in Pattison 2015).

20. 'Watercolour Guitars' (1998). Ian Peel writes that 'Watercolour Guitars is an ethereal McCartney guitar line, with Youth's trademark spacey bleeps coming in and out' (Peel 2000: 169), which is a good description of McCartney's profound engagement with ambient music. In this track, he takes a deep dive into the experimental. 'Watercolour Guitars' typifies the confidence of McCartney's monumental experimental trilogy via his electronica alter-ego The Fireman: *Strawberries Oceans Ships Forest* (1993), *Rushes* (1998) and *Electric Arguments* (2008). 'Watercolour Guitars' is an artistic kaleidoscope of neo-psychedelia, new age, ambient, dub, trip hop and trance.

Richard Mills
St Mary's University, London, UK
richard.mills@stmarys.ac.uk

Bibliography

Doyle, Tom (2013) *Man on the Run: Paul McCartney in the 1970s* (Edinburgh: Polygon).

Feldman-Barrett, Christine (2021) *A Women's History of the Beatles* (New York: Bloomsbury).

Jackson, Peter (dir.) (2021) *The Beatles: Get Back*.

The Late Show with Stephen Colbert (2019) 'Paul McCartney Often Dreams of John Lennon' [video], YouTube, 24 September 2019, https://www.youtube.com/watch?v=sPBTn746v4I (accessed 27 June 2022).

Norman, Philip (1981) *Shout!* (New York: MJF Books).

Pattison, Louis (2015) 'Paul McCartney's "McCartney II" turns 35 years old: how it foretold the sound of 1980s pop', NME Blogs, 15 May 2015, https://www.nme.com/blogs/nme-blogs/paul-mccartneys-mccartney-ii-turns-35-years-old-how-it-foretold-the-sound-of-1980s-pop-17280 (accessed 27 June 2022).

Peel, Ian (2002) *The Unknown Paul McCartney: McCartney and the Avant-Garde* (Richmond: Reynolds and Hearne).

Rice, Tim and Paul McCartney (1980) 'Paul McCartney Interview Tim Rice 1980 "Meet Paul McCartney"' [video], YouTube, recorded 8 August 1980, uploaded by Graham72 on 2 December 2020, https://www.youtube.com/watch?v=xm5Hs2MhzOk (accessed 24 June 2022).

Wenner, Jann (1971) *Lennon Remembers* (San Francisco: Straight Arrow Books).

Whiteley, Sheila (2000) *Women and Popular Music: Sexuality, Identity and Subjectivity* (London: Routledge).

Reviews

My Private Lennon: Explorations from a Fan Who Never Screamed
Sibbie O'Sullivan
Columbus: Ohio State University Press, 2020
ISBN: 9780814277577, 184 pp.

The weathered rockist skin is beginning to shed not only from male considerations of the rock narrative and the Beatles, but from female considerations too, and women are moving towards no longer needing to explain themselves as knowledgeable fans. Sibbie O'Sullivan illustrates this perfectly in her autoethnographic book *My Private Lennon: Explorations from a Fan Who Never Screamed*. She not only speaks to the Lennon fans, but bares her fandom and her version of Lennon for all, sharing life experiences and clearing a path for other women and fans to do the same.

My Private Lennon is not a weighty theoretical piece that takes days or weeks to trudge through: rather it is an intimate, fun, charming, witty and, mostly, quick read. What can slow this particular text down is the number of times you will stop and reflect on your own fandom: who the Beatles were and are to *you* and how you handle new information that may 'disrupt' or 'expand' your understanding of the Beatles and thus yourself (O'Sullivan 2021: 48). She explores intimate life experiences in considering her friendships, marriage, motherhood, and fandom — a beautifully woven tapestry of her little 'h'-histories and big 'H'-histories intertwined with *her* Lennon and Beatles.

O'Sullivan makes it clear that the Beatles she writes about are *hers* (183), and *her* Lennon will not be yours. From her Beatle beginning, she felt a connection to 'truth' over 'beauty' (102), and John Lennon was *her* truth. In no way does she dismiss the other Beatles, but with John she 'felt a recondite tribal pull' (28). This is evident

The Journal of Beatles Studies Autumn (2022)

ISSN 2754-7019 (online)
https://doi.org/10.3828/jbs.2022.9

throughout each essay as she invites the reader into different times in her history, in which she makes sense of her own life events by considering and connecting various threads of John's life.

Yet in this memoir, O'Sullivan not only revisits or recovers memories embedded deeply in Lennon fandom, but she revives and evolves with it — reimagining and releasing herself, and in a way all fans will recognize. She beautifully emblazons her fandom, wearing it with pride. Her description of being a fan is one that is relatable and reminds one that moments of meaning made from life events, such as seeing the Beatles live, are indelible. Her description of fandom will resonate with many:

> Being a fan is like floating down a long river: some banks have lush vegetation, some are strewn with beer bottles, some are for sunbathing, around the next one there's a lovely sunset. The point is to *know* the river, to dip your foot in it as many times as it takes to feel it as it moves along, which it will do with or without you. (33)

For O'Sullivan, it is evident she has stepped in and out of her river, as she finds John, or John finds her, at various parts of her life.

In her early days of fandom, O'Sullivan firmly declares, she did not scream, she 'oozed' (27), and after this declaration, she will no longer need to defend her fandom — something that benefits all fans and expressions of fandom. However, throughout the book and in the title, she distances herself from screaming Beatles fans, reminding us that our freedom to be fans in the open is still not quite free; that female fans, or Beatles fans in general, who understand that screams, then and now, are more than just sexual expression, must be defended. It is interesting that screaming has become a complexly negative stereotype, and O'Sullivan, who most likely knows that the screams were more than the commonly understood sexual hysteria, does not want to be associated with them. Many fans who screamed are challenging this narrative, and claim it was a way to express their love, such as Debbie Gendler and Carol Tyler (2021), and Christine Feldman-Barrett, who thoughtfully addresses this in *A Women's History of the Beatles* (2021). It seems that for O'Sullivan, asking someone, or at least herself, if she 'screamed' is equivalent to asking a woman who cannot have, or does not want, children,

'When are you having a baby?' However, she is not wrong in arguing that whether one screamed should not be the first question asked, if asked at all. While screaming was and is important to individuals for many reasons, it does not *make* a first-generation female Beatle fan — and this book epitomizes that idea.

At times, O'Sullivan appears protective of *her* John, illustrated by her criticisms of Yoko's display of John's bloody glasses (the glasses he was wearing when he was murdered) as well as charging admission to see Lennon artefacts — something she would not have done with *her* John's material possessions. She argues that the use of certain artefacts 'panders to those fans who see Lennon not as a man but as a religious deity' (87). Yet for many fans, there was not a chance to see the Beatles live. It is possible that museum exhibitions and artefacts (whether it be videos, glasses, clothing, guitars, bedrooms, etc.) are equivalent to the photograph of John she was lucky enough to take. Her discussion of Lester Bangs and the other rockist 'boys' further illuminates this when she refers to Bangs as 'pudgy' and suggests that without the Beatles he would have 'remained just another syrup head dying from an overdose' (15–16). It is easy to empathize with such comments, as our inner fandom moves to defend when what we admire is insulted. However, O'Sullivan felt the need to go beyond defending the Beatles, to criticize Bangs — as females are often criticized (think Yoko Ono and Linda McCartney). She reminds us that many fans have a profound or sacred relationship with our fandom, and hers clearly runs deep, but her comments about Yoko's decisions and about Bangs, several decades later, further shows how fandom, while full of love and admiration, can be cruel, subjective and protective. Anger at the wounds that critics (rock, family, friends or random individuals) have inflicted do not heal easily. However, after putting rock critics in their place, she sets herself free from the chains of what a female Beatles fan was, is, or should be, thus freeing all to be equal Beatles fans — whether one was 'there' or not.

Ultimately, it is not only O'Sullivan or John who is deeply present throughout the book, but oneself as a Beatles fan, and her baring her fandom to all, is not only for her, but for all fans. She reminds us that our perceptions matter, as she takes meaning from the man presented to her as art, not just a creator of art. Art has its flaws, its mysteries, and is seldom perfect — that is what makes it human and relatable. Just as her life is not perfect, she recognizes that John, as a man, lacked perfection, but the effect of and meaning made from her experiences with John and his work have shaped and helped make sense of her life — and really that is what this book is about. It is about sharing *her* story in relation to her fandom, a story that will be of interest to many who have their own experiences with John, Paul, George, Ringo, Elvis, Spock, Diana Ross, David Cassidy, Michael Jackson, the Spice Girls, Beyonce or Harry Potter. There is a growing academic interest in Beatle fandom such as Richard Mills's *The Beatles and Fandom: Sex, Death and Progressive Nostalgia* (2019), Kenneth Womack and Kit O'Toole's 2021 collection, *Fandom and the Beatles: The Act You've Known for All These Years* and Feldman-Barrett's *A Women's History of the Beatles* (2021), all of which consider what it means to be a female Beatles fan. O'Sullivan's text will only further the conversation beyond academia and is a beginning of what is to come, because other fans want to share and hear about individual experiences. *My Private Lennon* will undoubtedly encourage the embracing of fandom and inspire many to contribute their stories to cultural history, and to share *their* personal Jesus, John, or their private whomever.

Allison Bumsted
Austin Community College, Austin, Texas, U.S.A.
allisonbumsted@gmail.com

Bibliography

Feldman-Barrett, Christine (2021) *A Women's History of The Beatles* (New York: Bloomsbury).
Gendler, Debbie and Carol Tyler (2021) 'I Was a Teenage Screamer "It Was about Love!"' [video], excerpt from 'I Was Teenage Screamer' panel moderated by Allison Bumsted at Fab4ConJam, 21 February 2021, YouTube, uploaded by Robert Rodriguez, 19 February 2022, https://www.youtube.com/watch?v=WshAuAveXUc (accessed 18 August 2022).

Mills, Richard (2019) *The Beatles and Fandom: Sex, Death and Progressive Nostalgia* (New York: Bloomsbury).

Womack, Kenneth and Kit O'Toole (eds) (2021) *Fandom and the Beatles: The Act You've Known for All These Years* (New York: Oxford University Press).

Leadership Lessons with The Beatles: Actionable Tips and Tools for Becoming Better at Leading
Shantha Mohan
Abingdon: Routledge, 2022
ISBN: 9781032212562, 286 pp.

There are hundreds of books in different languages about the Beatles, most of them written by journalists, musicians, historians or other social scientists, and dealing with the history of the group or its members. We can verify the attraction and global cultural impact of the Beatles through recent sources, such as Peter Jackson's docuseries *The Beatles: Get Back*, the Rock & Roll Hall of Fame's recent exhibition, the miniseries *McCartney 3, 2, 1*, or the best sellers *The Lyrics: 1956 to the Present*, by Paul McCartney (Penguin, 2021), and *The Beatles: Get Back*, edited by John Harris (Callaway Arts & Entertainment, 2021).

But Shantha Mohan is not a musicologist or music historian; she holds a PhD in Operations Management, and has an undergraduate degree in Electronics and Communication. Her new book, *Leadership Lessons with The Beatles: Actionable Tips and Tools for Becoming Better at Leading*, focuses on leadership. It offers advice and tips, techniques and methods to achieve personal goals in the world of business management. In a recent interview for *India Currents*, she revealed that this book was in her mind for years, but found the time 'to put pen to paper' only after retiring from the company she co-founded, Retail Solutions Inc.

The author confesses to being 'a self-help junkie', and throughout sixteen chapters divided into four parts, she quotes famous writers of the genre like Carnegie, Seligman, Collins, Goleman, Ellis and Dryden. However, this is by no means a traditional self-help book. In *Leadership Lessons with The Beatles* Mohan links the characteristics of modern humanistic leadership with different ideas taken from various Beatles song lyrics, so each chapter has the title of a well-known song composed by the Fab Four.

In addition, she offers information on the songs to which she refers. For example, in the first chapter, 'Getting Better', she points out that the song was released in 1967, mentioning some of the instruments that accompany the melody (such as the Indian tambura played by George Harrison), highlighting the words of enthusiasm and optimism that Paul McCartney wrote, opposed to the melancholic and sorrowful contribution of John Lennon as a consequence of his 'dark past'. The author links the song 'Getting Better' with what she considers to be one of the most important characteristics of great leaders: optimism. Quoting Melinda Gates with reference to Warren Buffett: 'His success is not the reason he is optimistic. Instead, his optimism made him successful.' Subsequently, Mohan shares some ideas for building optimism in aspiring leaders.

Similarly, the following chapters expand the topics of humility (displayed in the song 'Within You, Without You'), the harsh journey of a leader ('The Long and Winding Road'), the virtue of curiosity that leads to 'better decision-making' ('Get Back'), and remembering that 'even leaders need help' ('Help!'). Similarly, she reflects on the need for a leader as an independent thinker, via 'Think for Yourself'; and 'I Want to Tell Tell You' points out that 'leaders are successful only when they can express their thoughts well'. 'We Can Work It Out' inspires Mohan's negotiation and conflict resolution experiences. Lastly her thoughts on how to deal with stress are reflected in the lyrics of 'Let It Be'. Each chapter is based on this same structure: introduction; brief comment on the song in question; development of the topic (which includes bibliographical references, as well as her own experiences as executive of various companies); summary; practice; 'questions to ask yourself'; and list of references.

Although she uses some very common phrases (such as the 'Serenity Prayer': 'God, grant me the serenity to accept the things I cannot change...'), in general this text is well written, well structured, with direct language for the general public. It is entertaining, and it adequately combines music and various models to consolidate leadership. Perhaps the only objection I can make to the author is that, as a male, I felt somewhat excluded from the dialogue, since throughout the book she only uses the personal pronoun 'she' (for instance: 'Think of a leader you like. Is she an excellent communicator? I bet she is'), instead of including inclusive terms such as she/he.

In summary, Shantha Mohan presents to us a book with a practical side, with useful ideas to develop leadership; but it is also a book about the importance of music in our lives: the social action it generates, nostalgia, emotions and the emotional intelligence, the positive and tangible values that music teaches us, and the inspiration and motivation that the music of the Beatles still spread. Not surprisingly, in the aforementioned book *The Lyrics,* Paul McCartney declares that 'people stop me in the street and they can get very emotional. They said "your music changed my life", and I know what they mean — that the Beatles brought something very important to their lives.' Mohan's book is a good example of how the music of the Beatles, even today, continues to change lives.

Luis Díaz-Santana Garza
Autonomous University of Zacatecas, Mexico
luis.diaz@uaz.edu.mx

John & Yoko/Plastic Ono Band
John Lennon and Yoko Ono; edited by Simon Hilton
London: Thames and Hudson, 2020
ISBN: 9780500023433, 288 pp.

John & Yoko/Plastic Ono Band is a Thames and Hudson publication that falls into the category of a coffee-table book due to its size, weight and high-quality paper stock and printing. Whilst I first assumed that this book would have a great deal in common style-wise with the photography book *Linda McCartney: Life in Photographs* (2011) by presenting the reader with lustrous, large-format photography of John Lennon and Yoko Ono's time as part of the Plastic Ono Band, it actually offers a lot more in the way of narrative and first-hand interview content from Lennon, Ono and others involved. A sizeable portion of the book is indeed dedicated to high-quality photography, but the structure and presentation of this book is not like a photography retrospective or even a historical reference book. This book is written like a documentary.

John & Yoko is not an academic book in its remit. It is a book for collectors and enthusiasts to effuse about when discussing its candid imagery and anecdotal stories interlaced with pages of handwritten lyrics and sketches. This it achieves with great success. However, in order to achieve flow and readability, a large number of the anecdotes and interview quotations remain un-referenced with regard to when and where the interviews or stories were told. As noted, *John & Yoko* is not a reference book, and therefore has no responsibility to provide me, as an academic, with this information. But as a Beatles obsessive and completist, as I assume are a good proportion of the target audience for this book, I am eager to follow a trail into the archives and, unfortunately, these signposts are not provided a great deal of the time. This unfettered presentation of intermingled interviews and stories adds to the 'quick cut' documentary feeling of talking heads and interviews, so what is lost in minutiae is more than gained in readability and entertainment. By leaving out interview sources, the editor was able to tell the story in a much more fluid and uncluttered manner and it did keep me interested and absorbed throughout.

Written rather strikingly up the edge of the closed pages of the book is the question 'Who are the Plastic Ono Band?' This question is not just a tease to the answer that lies inside. Rather, it acts as the central thesis of the whole piece, a thesis that pre-dates Christopher Small's famous 'musicking' concept by approximately thirty years but fully embodies its essence (Small 1998). In the preface, Yoko Ono Lennon lays out that 'the concept of the Plastic Ono Band was "the message is the music." So everyone on the recording is in it, everyone who sings the song is in it, you're in it and everyone in the world is in it' (13). This concept of inclusion in the Plastic Ono Band is extremely well covered in the opening chapter of the book and does show that the Ono Lennons had extremely forward-thinking ideas when it came to discussing audience reception and interaction in 1968, when their prime objective was the spreading of a message. By creating a culture of inclusion and including their audience in the musicking of their peace message, they were able to market peace in the way they wanted. John and Yoko's 'You are the Plastic Ono Band' concept of musicking was just as broad as Small's given that, according to Yoko, even I am in the Plastic Ono Band by 'listening to the recording', just as '[paying] attention in any way to a musical performance, including a recorded performance ... is to music' (Small 1998: 9). It is therefore interesting to see how audience engagement, and a consideration of reception, was at the core of what made the Plastic Ono Band more than just backing musicians (or a stage full of plastic objects and tape machines). This book, alongside the obvious heritage and fandom aspects of its release, details that the music released was intended more as an expression of *the message* than as commercial content.

The contents of the book are set out as a discography, with chapters or sections marked by song titles or single releases. If you were to browse this book and use the contents page as a reference for what is inside, then you might be forgiven for assuming it to be akin to books such as Steve Turner's *A Hard Day's Write* (1994) or Paul Du Noyer's *John Lennon: The Complete Songs* (2020), where the stories are quite specific with reference to lyrical content, inspiration, and so on. Instead, *John & Yoko* moves very smoothly through the chapters in a way that steers away from a formulaic reference text, and functions more like a continuous and well-told story. Yes, there are lyrics pages, and 'Cold Turkey' does come with the specific drug detox story with which it is associated, but the interweaving of story, pictures, lyrics and timeline is far broader and more encompassing than the contents page would have you believe. There is no narrative voice in this book, which I believe adds to the observational documentary feel of the overall piece.

This aspect of the text really does more to heighten the enjoyment of the content, whilst possibly reducing its 'researchability' from an academic perspective.

In this review, I have extolled the book's storytelling through its combination of interviews, photography and handwritten notes, and I think that its quality of entertainment and storytelling is key to why this book shines. And though I have stated my preference for more traceable referencing where interviews are concerned, my stance as an academic is not a negative one. The content in *John & Yoko/Plastic Ono Band* is interesting, informative and goes a lot deeper than I would normally expect from a coffee-table book. The book provides insight into the processes and mindsets of all those involved in the creation of the Plastic Ono Band and does so in a clear and accessible manner. It offers important first-hand insights into the music making and lives of John Lennon and Yoko Ono at the time and explains the core of their message and intentions. This is a valuable book for that reason alone. That said, it offered me more than I ask for as a collector and fan and goes most of the way to satisfying me as a researcher.

Taran Harris
University of Liverpool, U.K.
taran.harris@liverpool.ac.uk

Bibliography

Du Noyer, Paul (2020) *John Lennon: The Complete Songs* (London: Welbeck Publishing Group).

McCartney, Mary, Paul McCartney, Stella McCartney, Linda McCartney, Martin Harrison and Annie Leibovitz (2011) *Linda McCartney: Life in Photographs* (Cologne: Taschen).

Small, Christopher (1998) *Musicking: The Meanings of Performing and Listening* (Middletown, CT: Wesleyan University Press).

Turner, Steve (1994) *A Hard Day's Write: The Stories Behind Every Beatles Song* (New York: Harper Perennial).

The Lyrics: 1956 to the Present
Paul McCartney; edited with an Introduction by
Paul Muldoon
New York: Liveright Publishing Corporation, 2021
ISBN: 9781324091134, 912 pp.

When asked by host John Wilson of the BBC's *This Cultural Life* (2021) podcast why he had never written a proper autobiography, Paul McCartney responded: 'It's a lot of work.' This understatement, along with being characteristically pithy, resonates with McCartney's philosophy toward making music. During a discourse on his goofy fan favourite 'Temporary Secretary' in his new book *The Lyrics: 1956 to the Present*, McCartney muses: 'People often say, "Oh, you work so hard," and I say, "We don't work; we play"' (706).

McCartney, the most successful songwriter of this or any other age, is the ultimate musical adventurer, an artist who follows his playful instincts wherever they may take him and rarely if ever gets sidetracked by doubt. When asked to write an orchestral piece for the 150th anniversary of the Royal Liverpool Philharmonic Orchestra, it did not even occur to McCartney to be intimidated by the task; in fact, he was puzzled by the idea that anyone even thought he would be intimidated. In *The Lyrics*, in which each set of song lyrics is accompanied by McCartney's commentary (edited for clarity and consistency by the poet Paul Muldoon), the composer of the *Liverpool Oratorio* asks — rhetorically but sincerely — 'You have to know how to do things in order to do them?' (205).

In addition to being one of the twentieth century's leading songwriters and musicians, Paul McCartney excels at the art of the interview. Of the four Beatles, none has ever been as game for a stroll down memory lane, not to mention a bit of easy publicity. So it should not be surprising that the closest thing to an autobiography that McCartney has yet produced originated as a series of conversations with Muldoon, which the poet then transcribed, edited and arranged into an alphabetical journey through McCartney's entire career as a songwriter — or as much of it as McCartney has seen fit to rehash. There are a few notable omissions from the Beatles era, and to include every song McCartney wrote outside the group, alone and collaboratively, would require a book three times the size of Liveright's, which on its own comprises over 900 pages of lyrics, commentary, photographs, documents and artefacts spanning McCartney's entire lifetime. The MPL archives have been more or less ransacked for this huge souvenir set; reading the book is like wandering through a McCartney-themed museum with the subject as your tour guide. In a sense, *The Lyrics* is the ultimate McCartney interview: all the stories he's told over the course of fifty years, compiled alongside his life's work.

Reading the lyrics on their own, separate from the music, is an unnatural act for a Beatles fan. Beatles songs are musical above all else; if fans learned anything about the band's songwriting process from the Peter Jackson documentary *The Beatles: Get Back* — released in November 2021, likely to purposely coincide with *The Lyrics* — it is that Lennon and McCartney's lyrics were written to serve the melody and the groove, not the other way around. Nevertheless, taken as poetic artefacts, arranged in stanzas and with line breaks, McCartney's lyrics show the songwriter's intuitive understanding of rhythm and metre. Take the first entry in the book, 'All My Loving' (2–7). This song is famous for so many other things — Lennon's propulsive rhythm guitar, Harrison's country-flavoured solo, being the first song the band played on their historic *Ed Sullivan Show* debut — that the lyrics are rarely treated as more than mere window dressing. But seeing them laid out on the page rather than hearing them sung, we notice the poetical aspects. The verse is written in perfect anapaests (where stresses appear on every third syllable), and the song follows an unusual *aabccb* rhyme scheme, an atypical one for rock and roll. For a songwriter who was not yet 21 years old at the time of the song's composition, McCartney shows a remarkable feel for the mechanics of the English language. There are, of course, outliers: the deep cut 'I Wanna Be Your Man', whose title is repeated no fewer than eighteen times over the course of the song, looks perfectly ridiculous written out in verse.

Of the conspicuous omissions made by *The Lyrics*, a few are worth noting. You won't find 'Oh! Darling' or 'I'm Looking Through

You' or 'Getting Better' represented, though the last of these was likely left out due to the unfortunate and uncharacteristic allusion to spousal abuse in the final verse. Given these notable absences, some of the selections chosen to represent the Beatles era are curious. The songs that conclude the *Abbey Road* suite, for instance — 'Golden Slumbers', 'Carry That Weight' and 'The End', plus the band's shortest-ever song, 'Her Majesty' — have full entries devoted to them, despite each one having only a few lines of lyrics. ('The End' maxes out at four.) To McCartney's credit, he has no problem finding stories and associations for even the most diminutive entries in his oeuvre. 'Golden Slumbers', for instance, offers one of several opportunities for McCartney to share memories of his father, Jim, a character whose presence in the book is rivalled only by John Lennon and Linda McCartney. Even 'The End', a whole twenty-six words of text, inspires a discourse on the art of the poetic couplet, invoking the names of Shakespeare, Chaucer, Alexander Pope and Wilfred Owen. The couplet at the end of 'The End', as it happens, is set in iambic tetrameter, making the discussion of these great poets particularly apt. The same entry features McCartney's musings over what might have become of him if he'd followed a literary career path rather than a musical one. The reader may wince at the thought of the twentieth century being deprived of one of its artistic pillars in favour of a middling academic, but this brief detour reminds us that there was a burden to being in the Beatles — 'a band that rather took over my life', as McCartney writes at the end of this chapter (165). The thought of a member of the most celebrated band of all time wondering what might have been reminds us that no matter what we pursue in life, and no matter how fulfilling or lucrative that path, we always leave behind a life — or two, or several — not lived.

The choice to list the entries alphabetically may not seem unusual at first glance. If the goal is to create a sort of McCartney encyclopaedia, alphabetical would be the default order of things. However, if *The Lyrics* is, as the front matter insinuates, a sort of musical autobiography, it is worth wondering why the material of the book is not presented chronologically. The book jacket claims that arranging the titles by letter allows for a 'kaleidoscopic rather than a chronological account' of McCartney's life. That is a neat bit of rhetorical gymnastics, but it does not quite explain why this arrangement is intuitive for telling a life story. The order of the letters of the alphabet is, after all, arbitrary; Samuel Taylor Coleridge once compared an alphabetical encyclopaedia to scattered fragments of knowledge, 'like a mirror broken on the ground' (Moran 2020). Not quite a kaleidoscope, then, since those at least have symmetry. A chronological catalogue would allow the backdrop of McCartney's life to unfold naturally against the songs, whereas the alphabetical one forces our esteemed narrator — not to mention our surely overburdened editor — to jostle between anecdotes, rarely following a single thread for more than a full page of text.

Such a complaint, though, implies that the average reader is going to approach *The Lyrics* like any other book, to be read from cover to cover without skipping ahead or doubling back. Some readers may indeed do so, but it is more likely that *The Lyrics* will be treated by fans as a reference work. And though as a lyrical reference it is far from complete — the collection comes nowhere close to containing every lyric McCartney has written — it is as a compilation of stories and anecdotes, both well-worn and lesser known, that this collection earns its price tag. Beatles fans can recite more than a few of the stories included in this volume as catechism, a circumstance not hurt by the fact that McCartney never tires of telling them. The stories behind 'Hey Jude' and 'Yesterday' are canonical texts in Beatledom, as are such core memories as the first meeting between Lennon and McCartney. Even more obscure stories that appear in *The Lyrics*, such as McCartney being awakened to the horrors of the Vietnam War during a chat with Bertrand Russell, have been public record for years. As with any reference collection, the value of *The Lyrics* lies not in its revelations but in its comprehensiveness. A book this big, expensive and frankly heavy (8.6 lbs according to Amazon) ought to be the last book you will ever need on its subject. Given its autobiographical scope — stretching from McCartney's childhood to the COVID-19 pandemic; reproducing on glossy paper nearly every photo and artefact in the MPL vaults; compiling stories about nearly every person of note that the author has ever had a cup of tea with — *The Lyrics* may be the rare book to satisfy such a daunting demand.

Michael R. Fisher
Rowan University, Glassboro, NJ, U.S.A.
fisherm@rowan.edu

Bibliography

Jackson, Peter (dir.) (2021) *The Beatles: Get Back.*
Moran, Joe (2020) '*A Place for Everything* by Judith Flanders — the curious history of alphabetical order', *The Guardian*, 30 January 2020, https://www.theguardian.com/books/2020/jan/30/a-place-for-everything-by-judith-flanders-the-curious-history-of-alphabetical-order (accessed 21 August 2022).
Wilson, John (host) (2021) 'Paul McCartney' [podcast episode], *This Cultural Life*, BBC Radio 4, 30 December 2021, https://www.bbc.co.uk/programmes/m0010wp3 (accessed 21 August 2022).

Printed and bound by CPI Group (UK) Ltd, Croydon, CR0 4YY

13/04/2025

14656600-0001